Praise for *Building a Winning Team:*
The Power of a Magnetic Reputation and the Need to Recruit
Top Talent in Every School

"Talent manifests within the culture of organizations when the formative outcomes align with the vision of what doors education will offer our students throughout their lives. Talented teachers ensure this happens on a daily basis. If you want to recruit talented educators who will change the culture of your school and attract more talent, read *Building a Winning Team*!"

—**Dennis Griffin Jr.**, principal and speaker

"Throughout my career, I have seen some amazing teams in the NBA. It takes a special skill to build and maintain a winning team! This book tells you just how to do that! *Building a Winning Team* is a must-read for every leader and coach of any organization."

—**Marc Zumoff**, 76ers play-by-play analyst on NBC

"There just aren't enough books available that are written for practitioners by practitioners that include both the research and the evidence to support new ways for leading schools. As a principal, I have found that teacher turnover is a growing issue. Joe, Salome, and T.J. spend no time admiring the problems we face. They jump right into solutions with tips, spotlights, and leadership team activities. Not only did I read this book, but I plan on using it as a blueprint to improve the reputation of my school along with the recruitment tactics we use to find great staff members. I've read their work for years, I've seen them speak, and they hit the nail on the head again with *Building a Winning Team*. Love it!"

—**Cynthia Jewell**, principal, Stockbridge Elementary School, Georgia

"There are so many accessible and actionable ideas in these pages, focused not only on attracting and retaining talent but creating a culture where educators and students excel and grow, while tapping into and bringing out their gifts to make schools a better place for all. An incredible read that I will be suggesting to leadership teams over and over again."

—**George Couros**, international speaker and author of *The Innovator's Mindset* and *Innovate Inside the Box*

"The most successful schools are those who are able to attract and retain the best educators. They do so through belief, instilling a sense of purpose, and consistent support. Creating this type of culture that people want to be a part of is a secret no more as Joseph Jones, Salome Thomas-EL, and T.J. Vari provide a blueprint, backed by pertinent examples as experiences from the trenches. The ideas and strategies presented will help you in your quest to unlock the potential of your team."

—**Eric Sheninger**, best-selling author and senior
fellow with the International Center for Leadership in Education

"As a teacher and coach with over 50 years of experience in public education, I've been a part of many great teams and I know that teamwork begins with leadership. Great leaders, like great coaches, invest in their people, develop their skills, and always put students first. This is a powerful book on how to build a winning team filled with proven, practical ideas."

—**Jim Doody**, educator

"Creating a star lineup in our schools and organizations is a goal of all leaders. Authors Jones, Thomas-EL, and Vari have provided ideas, reflections, and recommendations that help leaders assemble great teams. They bring value, importance, and suggestions to recruit top talent, establish the culture, and carefully select the best candidates. Useful tools are busting out of every chapter. *Building a Winning Team* is a must read for anyone working in a team environment."

—**Connie Hamilton**, curriculum director, speaker,
and author of *Hacking Questions*

"Future Ready principals are able to build great teams and create cultures of support and innovation. In *Building a Winning Team*, the authors do an incredible job of providing real-life examples for readers and relevant solutions to one of our most prominent issues in education. The future of our teachers, schools, and students will depend on how well we recruit the best to join our teams. This book should be on the reading list of every leader."

—**Thomas C. Murray**, director of innovation,
Future Ready Schools, Washington, DC

"As a consultant who has had the honor to work with thousands of schools globally, I believe that nothing has a greater impact on student performance than a winning team of educators and administrators. Winning school teams attract top talent and create a culture of success that benefits both students and staff. Dr. Joseph Jones, Dr. Salome Thomas-EL, and Dr. T.J. Vari have authored a book that is a blueprint for building a winning team. It is a must read for any administrator who aspires to build an impactful school culture."

—**Darrell "Coach D" Andrews**, education consultant
and author of *Believing The HYPE—Seven Keys To
Motivating Students of Color*

"As a leader learner in education, one of my priorities has always been assembling and supporting a dynamic team of educators who have a singular goal—doing what is in the best interest of all students! We know the relationships that develop in our classrooms impact everything from school-wide academic achievement to school culture and so recruiting and hiring innovative, thoughtful and passionate educators must always be our priority and the authors of *Building A Winning Team* have outlined the key steps and tools to accomplish this goal! If you want to build a winning team you need to read this book immediately!"

—**Dr. Tony Sinanis**, educator, author, and speaker

"In my role as a teacher and school principal, I see each day the importance of creating a great team. Building a culture that supports positive teamwork is the foundation of any good school. As leaders, it is important that we find great teachers and administrators for our students. The authors have given us the handbook for building winning teams. I think it is time we get to work! Please read *Building a Winning Team*. It will change how you lead!"

—**Dr. Amy Fast**, high school principal, author,
and education commentator

"Some books you read to learn, some simply transform our practice, giving us a comprehensive roadmap to navigate school leadership. In "Winning Teams" the authors have done an outstanding job highlighting the power of telling our story, making it a priority when developing our vision and brand. The questions and exercises will keep leaders in touch with the work, providing opportunities for deep reflection. No matter what stage of leadership you are in, there are strategies you will find valuable to grow your school, lead, and recruit winning teams!"

—**Lynn Colon**, director of English Learning Programs
and co-author of *Empower Our Girls*

"Taking their experience and success as leaders, the authors provide an outstanding resource for building a successful educational team and sharing information and resources that provide educational leaders the strategies to recruit the best of the best. The teacher shortage crisis across the U.S. is real. As educational leaders, it is more important than ever to find quality teachers who provide the passion and empathy for students and who will support the efforts of your district team. This is a must read for those of us who want nothing less than the best for our districts and most importantly, our students!"

—**Amber Heffner**, executive director, Illinois Digital
Educators Alliance

"As an assistant principal, I am most impressed by the candidates who can clearly explain the success they've had with building positive relationships with the students and parents they serve. This book will help me to build a winning team for sure. Every administrator should read *Building a Winning Team!*"

—**LaTonya Lonnise Harris**, EdD, assistant principal

"Jones, Thomas-EL, and Vari completely knocked it out of the stadium with this book. I've read hundreds of books and excerpts in my time as an educator—and *Building A Winning Team* is the complete educational bible that everyone needs!"

—**Adam Welcome**, educator, author, speaker, and Always Family First

Building a Winning Team

Building a Winning Team

The Power of a Magnetic Reputation and the Need to Recruit Top Talent in Every School

By Joseph Jones, Salome Thomas-EL, and T.J. Vari

ROWMAN & LITTLEFIELD
Lanham • Boulder • New York • London

Published by Rowman & Littlefield

An imprint of The Rowman & Littlefield Publishing Group, Inc.
4501 Forbes Boulevard, Suite 200, Lanham, Maryland 20706
www.rowman.com

6 Tinworth Street, London SE11 5AL, United Kingdom

British Library Cataloguing in Publication Information Available

Library of Congress Cataloging-in-Publication Data Available

ISBN 978-1-4758-4613-3 (cloth : alk. paper)
ISBN 978-1-4758-4614-0 (pbk. : alk. paper)
ISBN 978-1-4758-4615-7 (electronic)

♾™ The paper used in this publication meets the minimum requirements of American National Standard for Information Sciences—Permanence of Paper for Printed Library Materials, ANSI/NISO Z39.48-1992.

We dedicate this work to each of our winning teams. Our families inspire, support, and motivate us through their own talents and gifts. It is only through their belief in us and encouragement that we can do this important work in schools.

The Jones Team
Vicki
Nathan
Joey
Noah

The Thomas-EL Team
Shawnna
Macawi
Nashetah

The Vari Team
Andreina
Noah
Madison

Contents

Foreword

Throughout my career as a teacher and principal, I have always believed that great schools thrive when the culture consistently builds and supports a winning team, and great schools are always comprised of a tremendous staff. There is no substitute for a leader who takes full ownership of all that it means to carry the banner and create a positive school culture. The reality is that culture isn't something that happens by accident. It's an intentional, dogged, relentless, pursuit of excellence. Because exceptional school leaders realize that all of the "best practices" associated with thriving schools are most effective in a positive vibrant culture, they don't rest unless the team is "winning." In *Building a Winning Team*, you will learn that every touted educational practice related to student achievement is limited if the culture is not attuned to the needs of all students and the support and growth of all staff.

As I work with schools and districts across the country, I recognize more and more, that people desire a work environment where their leaders embrace the responsibility of building success within the organization. They want a workplace where excellence is expected and efficacy are front-and-center, and where the focus of the entire school community is on the well-being of every student as well as their academic achievement. When the culture is right, people will literally flock to your school and meet every expectation that you set. In this inspiring book, Principal EL, Joe, and T. J. have created a formula for every school to attract and retain high quality teachers, people who will stand out and ultimately contribute to the creation of a team that wins together every time.

Throughout this book, the authors discuss tough topics and offer readers a thorough breakdown of the problems and the solutions. The book dives right into the power of a school's reputation and how branding is not limited to the business world. They effectively argue that a school's story is going to be told by someone, but it is far more powerful if it is told by those in the trenches, the soldiers who are leading through all of its successes and failures each day. As I've always said, a school's story should accurately depict the truth in all of the great things that happen within its walls. The authors discuss the power of a school's reputation early in this must-read book, and they waste no time highlighting several critical areas of need for schools and what must be done by school leaders to make a difference immediately in their environment. As a merchant of hope myself, it is an honor to write this foreword and to support their work in creating positive energy and doing whatever it takes to champion for kids.

What I love about *Building a Winning Team* is that Principal EL, Joe, and T. J. describe some of the harsh conditions facing schools, especially those in high need areas, and they offer realistic solutions through their Deeper Dives, Technical Tips, and Leadership Team Activities. Readers will love their Practitioner Spotlights, which highlight leaders in the field who are getting results and doing the work that it takes to build their winning team. Readers will quickly connect with these stories, which inspired me as I read this book.

Lastly, this isn't just a book about teacher recruitment and retention. This book is about more than that. The focus is on building a superstar staff to change the lives of our students by hiring for excellence, but I found it to be mostly about culture. *Building a Winning Team* is about developing cultures where people can be their personal best for kids and where they want to stay for the long haul. Schools cannot flourish if they continue to suffer from a revolving door. Turnover in education impacts our students and it defeats our chances of assembling a great team. There are too many great people who want desperately to teach children, yet, find themselves discontent, frustrated, and eventually employed in a different profession. As a principal, I found that people always want to stay in their school and even do more when they feel valued, supported, and appreciated. Principal EL, Joe, and T. J. are not discouraged by the problems that we face in education with high teacher turnover and low morale, instead they offer solutions that you can put into practice today. Let's be innovative and develop reputations for our schools that stand out and communicate our sense of purpose. This book is inspiring and practical, and if you're looking to become a champion for all students and make a positive impact in your community, don't just read it, share the message with others. I am certain that after reading this book, you'll join the authors and myself on our journey to develop better school cultures and build winning teams in every school around the world.

—Jimmy Casas
Educator, speaker, leadership coach, and author of *Culturize*

Preface

The Growing Need for Talent

The need for talented teachers in schools is of critical importance for student learning and overall school culture. Research is clear with study after study demonstrating the power of highly effective teachers and their influence on student learning outcomes. In fact, in one study, the difference in student achievement between effective teachers and less effective teachers, on measures of both mathematics and reading performance, was found to be 30 percentile points (Strong, Ward, & Grant, 2011).

But teacher performance is not easily measured with quantifiable metrics, and there is little evidence that doing so using student test scores makes any bit of difference in elevating the profession (Darling-Hammond, 2013). With that said, the need for highly capable teachers is real, and talented teachers make a significant difference for students in both their learning and their desire to attend school.

Talent comes in many forms, and it presents as expertise, capacity, artistic, and powerful. Talented teachers change lives because of the "unique beliefs, values, attitudes, aspirations, motivation, knowledge, and skills" that they bring to the classroom (Strong, 2018). When we say "talented teachers," we're referring to teachers who make a difference for students through lasting relationships, intense learning experiences with proven outcomes, and positive influence on the school community. Truly talented teachers do all three—they build a relationship with students that literally lasts a lifetime, they make significant gains in student academic success, and they improve school culture through demonstrated leadership.

TALENT EQUATION MODEL

The challenge is that talented teachers aren't just ripe for the picking, out there growing on trees, making themselves available for schools by the dozens. The opposite is true with a 35 percent reduction in teacher education programming between 2009 and 2014. But that's not the most important factor in the talent equation. With an estimated loss of 8 percent of the workforce annually, attrition accounts for hundreds of thousands of nonretirement-age teachers leaving for any number of reasons (Sutcher, Darling-Hammond, & Carver-Thomas, 2016). Among the key factors in teacher turnover is a lack of administrative support. And although salary is accounted for as one of the top reasons why teachers leave the profession, the majority of their decision is based on preparation, support, and working conditions (Carver-Thomas & Darling-Hammond, 2017).

The costs are real in terms of hiring and replacement, but the student learning costs of teacher turnover far surpass the monetary problem. In addition, the numbers are even more bleak when considering minority teachers and the need for minority teaching candidates to serve our diverse student population (Paterson, 2018).

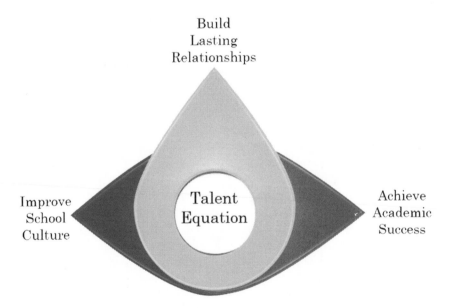

Figure 00.1. Talent Equation Model
Source: **Courtesy of Joseph Jones.**

The data is clear, with 44 percent of our elementary and secondary students coming from a minority background, while only 17.3 percent of the teaching population considers themselves of minority status (Ingersoll & May, 2016). The problem is exacerbated by the fact that although recruitment efforts have spiked with greater numbers of minorities entering the profession, these same minority teachers leave the profession at higher rates than their nonminority peers (Ingersoll & May, 2016).

The good news is that these problems with attracting teachers and recruiting quality educators do not need to persist. We have the power to shift the pattern, to alter the current reality by reworking the dynamics of the teaching experience, one school and one staff member at a time. This book is not about admiring the issues with teacher recruitment but rather the solutions and opportunities we have to make a difference for the future or our profession, from the inside out.

We believe that the answers are right within our grasp and well within our ability to enact change, which is why we wrote this book for any school leader who wants to alter the trajectory of his or her school by building a winning team. We hope that you find this work compelling, and, most of all, we hope that you find it useful. Allow us to describe a bit about what you'll find herein and within a subsequent book to come, called *Retention for a Change*, which we wrote as a companion piece to support your newly formed winning team.

For context, we include a fable about Pembroke High School, which you'll encounter twice in the book. The fable is designed as a through line to demonstrate the significance of a school's reputation and its active recruitment efforts. It also marks our transition from creating your reputation to active recruitment as leadership strategies in the creation of your best team ever. As features, chapters 3 and 9 each have a *deeper dive* into a specific practice that supports your winning team by developing a particular concept further and a *technical tip* that you can implement in your school right away.

Chapters 4, 5, 10, and 11 focus on the practical application of the ideas presented in the book and feature a "spotlight" that exemplifies the extraordinary efforts of real leaders in the field. Also within these chapters four leadership team activities are designed to help you take action so that you can develop your team and build the culture you desire for the future of your school.

All of the chapters end with either focus questions for you as a leader or guiding questions for your team. It's important to grapple with who, what, where, why, and how we move forward. Notice that we do not include "when." The *when* is now. In addition, you'll encounter key terms along the way, like "success practices," "teacher archetype," and "team study," which are all explained throughout the book and named so that you can put them into practice in your school. Finally, chapters 6 and 12 provide a "standing out" section that details a story of real success in terms of attracting and recruiting top talent in schools. As we conclude, you'll find one final story that we're sure will inspire you to build your winning team.

Acknowledgments

We want to thank our school and district teams. We would never be able to do this work without the inspiration, support, and insight of our peers and colleagues. We want to thank everyone who contributed to this work with stories and permissions; your practical experiences are what deepen the value in what it means to build a winning team. Finally, we would be remiss if we didn't thank our Delaware State Department of Education, the Delaware Association of School Administrators, and the Delaware Association of School Principals. The professional support network in our small state allows us to connect at a deep level with great people who do everything they can to strengthen school teams for the sake of student learning. We owe all of you a debt of gratitude for your vision, influence, and belief in schools.

Introduction

A Winning Team

The importance of having a talented teacher is above all else the single most distinguishable factor in student learning. Studies have demonstrated that approximately 20 percent of the differences in student success from classroom to classroom during any given year can be attributed to the teacher. Another 60 percent of the variance in learning is accounted for by the teachers that the student had in previous years (Scheerens & Bosker, 1997). This means that 80 percent of any difference made to student learning is directly associated with teacher selection and assignment and that effective teachers, over time, have a cumulative impact on outcomes.

Furthermore, studies demonstrate the drastic difference between having a highly effective teacher and having a low-performing one. In one study, the difference between having an effective teacher three years in a row and having a less-effective teacher three years in a row meant scoring at the 83rd percentile or the 29th (Sanders & Rivers, 1996). The problems with ensuring that students have multiyear experiences with talented teachers are due to the variability in the characteristics that teachers have as professionals. From special certifications to advanced degrees to focused in-service training, teachers vary in their skill set and ability to develop a dynamic learning environment for students (Whitehurst, 2002). This makes it all that much more important to attract talented teachers who bring a number of experiences and expertise to the equation, and it makes it imperative that we grow and motivate teachers whom we have in our systems already.

One feature that sets quality educational systems and individual schools apart from their underachieving neighbors is an ability to attract talented teachers to the system. This isn't left to chance as an arbitrary phenomenon. Instead, it's a deliberate and intentional endeavor on the part of the leaders within the system from both a human resources standpoint and the distinct desire to build a winning team for the sake of student success. And winning teams beget winning teams because the stronger the talent is on the team, the more likely the team is to attract more talented people.

Talented people want opportunities for growth more than anything else. The strongest, most successful workers, deepen their motivation through learning and professional development. Collins (2001) found that *good* companies spend a great deal of time working to motivate employees, while *great* companies don't consider motivation to be their role. Instead, they seek to hire people who are already motivated to do the work and dismiss those who aren't.

Research indicates that talented people are so motivated to grow that growth structures and growth planning are actually the best motivational strategies for retaining them (Gostick & Elton, 2007). But "the bottom line is that motivating people is paramount to a company's [or school's] ability to survive, perhaps even more important now than it has ever been before" (Gostick & Elton, 2007). This means that school leaders need ways to motivate teachers, and at the top of the list for the most talented among us is through growth opportunities. Furthermore, we need to attract and recruit already-motivated team members in ways that will not only add to our team of winners but also change the dynamics of the current team.

The reasons behind *why* we need talented teachers instructing our students are clear and abundant. The challenge schools face is *how* to attract and retain high-quality teachers. Essentially, we must create a system that ensures that an incredible teacher is instructing every student, every day. Although this is no easy task, there are ways to maximize the hiring process to enable school systems to build an organization filled with highly capable teachers, which is explored throughout this book.

To do so, school administrators must recognize that hiring is an ongoing process, not an event, with layers of influential practices. We liken the hiring process to the popular and proven effective, before, during, and after (BDA), reading strategy. Hiring excellent teachers requires key strategies that need to be employed similar to that of the BDA. *Before* students actually read, they should know the tenets of why they are going to read a particular piece and its relevance.Once this knowledge is established, they need to adopt key strategies to engage them with the text to help them monitor their understanding *during* reading. And finally, the *after* aspect of the strategy is designed to further engage readers and allow them to demonstrate what they've learned through a designed activity (Bergman & Schuler, 1992).

Just as a successful reader leverages reading strategies, successful administrators know how to use successful strategies within the three key aspects of the hiring process that we call the *BDA R3 Model*: (1) Develop a magnetic *reputation* that conveys your story and attracts talented teachers. (2) Actively *recruit* talented teachers using new and innovative human resources strategies. (3) *Retain* talented teachers with a motivational and inspirational culture that supports new hires as well as veterans.

Although each one is independent of the other and requires individual attention and support, successful school systems understand how each of the components functions together holistically. School leaders must understand how each one contributes to the success of the other and how all three work in harmony to develop a stable staff environment. School leaders who capitalize on each part of the *BDA R3 Model* process build a better hiring culture and a winning team. This book is dedicated to the first of the two Rs, *reputation* and *recruitment* efforts, which happen *before* and *during* the hiring process. You'll find the rest of the equation, which is the *after* hiring *retention* practices, in our forthcoming book, *Retention for a Change*, released in the coming months after this work. A last note on the title, *Building a Winning Team*—*these* words hold a significant meaning in that great leaders are always *building*, they create a *winning* mentality, and they treat everyone as a valued member of the *team*.

DEVELOPING YOUR REPUTATION

Attraction is about interest and curiosity, and for schools to draw the best candidates, they must cultivate an awareness among potential candidates that lures them into a desire to join the team. This occurs when schools share their story and create an authentic narrative regarding the tremendous work that is being done each day. This *reputation* aspect of hiring happens *before* you even have a vacancy and establishes what the school is about and the driving purpose behind the vision.

This concept is simple, but schools may face several barriers when developing a reputation. Candidates are drawn to various schools for a variety of reasons, such as higher pay, safety, location, teacher and administrative relationships, and niche roles. Of course, some schools, simply based on location, can attract or detract prospective teachers. The fact remains that many schools enjoy favorable circumstances that create better situations for administrators to select from a crop of talented candidates during any given hiring season. On the other hand, tons of schools operate in conditions that deter teachers from applying for open jobs.

There are schools that struggle to attract top talent and even find themselves desperate to fill vacant positions throughout the entire year with any teacher at all, let alone with the most qualified candidates. As Walsh, Putnam, and Lewis (2015) contend, "Recruitment and retention indisputably drive the inequitable distribution of the best teachers." This reality has disastrous effects on a school's overall success and contributes to poor student achievement, perpetuating only the negative circumstances that prevent teachers from applying in the first place.

But, contrary to typical school system human resource practices, attracting teachers actually begins *prior* to the act of recruiting them and is achieved by schools that create a compelling vision that paints a clear picture of what the school is about and what it strives to achieve. These ideals are the foundational elements that can successfully compete with the harsh conditions that prevent many prospective teachers from applying. And, often, without a proper reputation, an applicant might never even be aware of a school that he or she has within driving distance of his or her home. Schools that offer a vision that serves as the basis for *why* someone would want to work there create the positive reputation that helps build the winning team when a vacancy arises.

There are no quick-fix remedies that will solve a school's inability to create a stable staff filled with great teachers. Rather, *the fix* requires an honest and in-depth look at the school to uncover the truths that limit a school's success and the challenges that prevent it from attracting an elite staff. There are, on the other hand, best practices, guided by principles and strategies, which each chapter in this book uncovers so that you can begin making strides within the realm of recruiting your best team yet. Because attracting talent actually begins prior to filling a vacancy, the first chapters of this book cover four key areas with which schools must be obsessed about in order to attract incredible talent and yield greater success (Hansen, 2018):

1. Attract talent with a magnetic story that will compel others to join the team.
2. Create a school culture on the foundation of a clear and powerful vision.
3. Leverage core values to determine the guiding forces behind every decision to improve results.
4. Develop a teacher talent archetype that identifies precisely who you need to hire to be successful for stronger performance in the classroom.

Attracting teachers through a positive reputation that precedes any vacancy is only the first step. The second part of the process is actively recruiting and hiring top talent to be on the team.

RECRUITING TOP TALENT

There are several important phases to recruiting and hiring top talent. Too often, though, we think of hiring teachers and school personnel as something that happens at one point in time, such as the spring when teacher turnover is known to be high and school administrators begin their hiring process. Although the act of hiring predominantly occurs during specific times of the year, the mind-set among administrators and human resource personnel must change to view recruiting and hiring as an ongoing process with unique opportunities for the candidate, the existing staff, and the school.

Not only does hiring a new teacher fulfill a need due to a vacancy, but a well-developed process is also a great way to strengthen the school team. By actively recruiting, using unconventional methods and out-of-the-box think-ing, we can institute practices that find potential candidates whom we might not otherwise uncover. In doing so, we can also assure them that our school is the right one for them. This requires a new level of innovation with the need to incentivize candidates and advertise positions in uncommon ways.

The truth is that the traditional post-and-apply methods won't give you the applicant pool you desire. Having a keen understanding of what your school represents, and how it will invest in and support its teachers, is the primary tool for building your winning team, but it has to be active, engaging, and fun. Potential hires need to know that they are joining something special. Teaching is a phenomenal career, and we need to glamorize our jobs. The process of recruiting and hiring should be exciting and eventful, instilling in the candidate a desire to be on our team while building the current team at the same time.

In this book, we push the boundaries of what it means to actively engage your pool of candidates as well as what it means to use hiring as a tool to develop your current team. We'll take you through a series of new and dif-ferent interview tactics, better ways to approach hiring staff so that you can build your award-winning team. Four major themes emerge:

1. Be patient when looking to fill a vacancy to guarantee that you hire the perfect candidate for any particularly specialized role on the team.
2. Position yourself as a winner with new tactics to incentivize the vacancy through innovative thinking.
3. Leverage unorthodox recruiting and hiring methods with strategies to advertise positions far and wide to develop an exceptional team.
4. Develop a position archetype that identifies precisely what the school needs to be successful and then glamorize your hiring process so that it's fun for everyone involved.

Recruiting teachers is a huge step to developing your new and current team, but it's not the end goal. We often fail at motivation and retention because we confuse our efforts to recruit with what it really means to inspire the team. Motivating, inspiring, and energizing your staff are the only ways to retain them, but that happens *after* you've built the team. This book uncovers the reasons why we must change our approach to attracting and recruiting talent *before* and *during* our hiring process in order to be successful.

We dedicate our next book, *Retention for a Change*, to all of the motivational aspects of a winning team, which happens *after* you build it. As you uncover the first of the two Rs in our *BDA R3 Model* within this book, know that the third R has a significant influence on whether or not you keep your newly built team together. We challenge you to create a magnetic reputation; actively recruit talent in new ways; and then retain them through motivation, inspiration, and energy at work. Let's get started by learning why and how you should tell your story.

BUILDING A WINNING TEAM MODEL

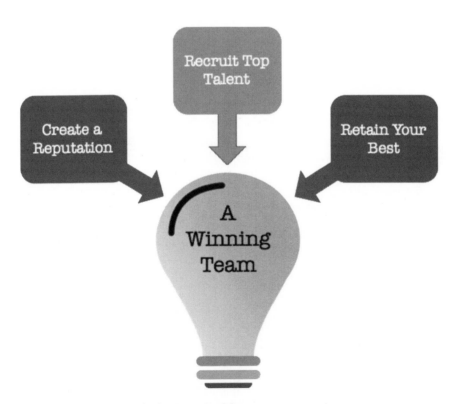

Figure 0.1.   Building a Winning Team Model
Source: **Courtesy of Joseph Jones.**

Chapter 1

The Magnetic Force of a School's Story

Any measuring stick worth its salt not only tells you where you stand, it also helps you decide what to do next.

—Buckingham and Coffman (1999, p. 40)

Pembroke High School, home to 1,372 students, 133 staff, and 3 administrators, is backed by an army of local support and high expectations. Pembroke is a pillar of possibilities and future opportunities, proudly centered within the town of Passel. Constructed in 1952, a nondescript building, lacking any grandiose architecture or remarkable features, is a testament to the postwar efforts to create modern schools for a booming generation with better lighting, improved ventilation, and well-designed classrooms.

What the school lacks in exterior characteristics can be found within the interior, among the staff and students, which is the embodiment of excellence. The building itself, although aging, is the pride and joy of the town and is meticulously kept, well manicured, and, for a lack of better words, sparkling clean. The school represents perseverance, values, and the belief that through education, lives can be improved and towns can survive anything.

The town of Passel has endured much of the turbulence that communities often face. Once a thriving manufacturing town that capitalized on the refrigeration era, Passel saw the industry downsize, jobs leave, and homes vacated. There were times when the community seemed beyond repair given their economic challenges and lack of business opportunities.

Despite any economic downturn and associated circumstances, the town kept education at the forefront and invested in its children as best as it could. Through it all, and for those who remained and rebuilt the economy and the community, Pembroke High remained the key to ensuring that students learned the necessary skills to be productive citizens and contributing members of the community.

The school evolved into the hub, and as new industries emerged and Passel's economic vitality grew, the school adapted and offered progressive classes that reflected the community's industries and economic needs. Over time, incredible scholars and skilled students graduated from the school, and the school received noteworthy accolades. Pembroke continued to embrace change, adapting and remaining agile, championing science and math while keeping true to its core values, never losing sight of its storied past.

Today, the school is considered an innovation lab where learning is actuated into systems and products. Students enjoy college and career pathways, which are dictated by the job market as well as social and political needs.

The school celebrates success and possibility every day. The school's administration and staff continually work to build strong partnerships with families, businesses, and local legislators. The alumni association is an active group, and the parent-teacher organization is progressive with its approach to funneling money back into the classrooms. The school's vision and values dominate decision-making, and the Pembroke brand is undeniable.

The motto "Every student is at the heart of every decision" creates clarity, focus, and a belief that students can and should enjoy learning. Because of such clarity and purpose, Pembroke attracts teachers and leaders from far and wide. Its reputation for staying strong and positive even in hard times generates publicity, accolades, and long lines to join the team.

While this narrative is a fable, it can be told about any school with a winning team and an attractive culture. Schools that cultivate the right mind-set from within never have a problem with their prestige, their prominence, or the magnetic force of their esteemed story.

STORY + PRIORITIES = ATTRACTION

The first tenet of this book is the simple fact that hiring starts long before a vacancy exists and needs to be filled. Schools and businesses alike need to be places where people want to belong, which draws the attention of prospective candidates. The most attractive workplaces have an identifiable and well-known culture that reaches far beyond the company walls.

This type of magnetic environment appeals to job seekers and sparks interest for those who desire a better work experience. A list of great places to work, found on Forbes.com and other sites, reveals similar themes in terms of employee engagement, inclusive environments, and programs that allow for personalization and flexibility (Gassam, 2018). And these themes are integral characteristics of great organizations that make it clear for everyone to see that their working environment is exciting and that their employees are valued as both contributors and people.

Companies with a positive and empowering culture on the inside ensure that everyone on the outside knows about it, which attracts potential candidates and deepens the pool for hiring. They tell their story, repeatedly, controlling the narrative. They do so because they know that if they don't champion their brand, it will diminish or someone else will portray a different message, painting an alternative picture about them.

This organizational messaging heralds the company name, evident through the product line and its purpose. It's an advertisement about what it means to be an employee and the benefits of working for a great organization with a fantastic work environment. Culturally identifying messages of this kind are generally told by anyone and everyone in the company, from executives at the top to those working in the field, whose message often resonates the most and travels the fastest.

Some leaders even promote their message within the vast literature on leadership, captivating readers through the power of storytelling by writing a book about their company and its culture. Tony Hsieh, CEO of Zappos, wrote *Delivering Happiness*, which explains how his emphasis on corporate culture led to unprecedented profits. Howard Stoeckel, then CEO of Wawa, is another great example of an executive who describes the power of family and culture and how to build a successful organization in his book *The Wawa Way*. He describes the company's origin, its core values, and how it attracts loyal employees, which it calls "associates."

The critical notion is that businesses that want to attract top talent take proactive steps to tell their story far and wide. Schools can take a page from the marketing expertise found in businesses, like Zappos and Wawa, by explicitly informing the community about all of the incredible work being done every day. Schools spend an enormous amount of time focusing on culture and student success and developing an environment that is supportive for all students.

That message needs to be clear for everyone to understand and know so that people gain a realistic and insightful picture of what is truly going on within the schoolhouse walls. If not, schools remain subject to someone else's narrative, which is not always favorable and misleads the public, which deters potential employees.

Your story is your reputation, and the truth is that your school's story *will* get told. Who tells it pervasively and consistently is the question. It can be told by people with whom you work, on a consistent and regular basis, or it can be told by others, who typically wait for those fleeting moments when something goes wrong.

One problem is that leaders often overestimate how well they are telling their story and how many employees are actually telling the story that they want them to tell. "Leaders are inherently biased to presume that everyone in the group sees things as they do, when in fact they don't" (Coyle, 2018). This means we have to double down on telling our school's story for two reasons: (1) First, we need to be more consistent and more robust in our messaging than anyone else who may want to tell their version of our story. (2) Second, we need to account for the fact that because we live out our story each day, we tend not to "feel" like it needs to be told. The truth is that the greater community does not know what is actually going on every day in your school.

Your school's story can be told in many ways and through a number of mediums, but the point is that it needs to be loud enough, pervasive enough, and consistent enough that it is well known and attractive. It must work to create your reputation on a regular and recurring basis. The most important of reasons is that hiring starts long before a vacancy occurs, and highly talented individuals are looking for opportunities for openings on a winning team, just so that they can be part of something special. Every school must tell its own special story.

Telling Your Story

Schools that thrive send clear messages and tell poignant stories that develop into a narrative of success that reveals their brand. This creates positive energy and enthusiasm, providing a community outlook that the school is an awesome place to work and learn. This also generates a buzz that your school deserves, attracting onlookers as they make decisions about their next place to apply. Hiring talented people and building a winning team depend on the reputation of your brand long before you have a vacancy available. The good news is that the prototype for building a winning brand by marketing your school is accessible as a model for you to use.

Great educators share their stories far and wide, day in and day out. We've heard from Beth Houf, coauthor of *Lead like a Pirate*, and Amber Teamann (who blogs at amberteamann.com). Both of these progressive principals are getting their school stories told through social media, blogging, and presenting so that their message is positive, celebratory, and, most important, coming from them. But the truth is that too many schools are still quiet, even worse, silent, when it comes to a social presence and creating attractiveness for the outside world.

Worse yet, we know of educators who have been stifled and forbidden from communicating without serious policy implications, laborious approvals, and technical filters. Although many are well meaning and we understand the intention of these provisions, they thwart and prevent our ability to share the fantastic happenings in schools. If you find yourself in this situation, being held back, even if your district has severe stipulations, and even if you can't afford the billboard space that you want for your message, you must overcome these obstacles and find creative ways so that your school stands out at the top of the list of places where new college graduates and current educators from all over the globe want to work.

Simply put, you need to create a competitive advantage so that potential candidates know your story, your priorities, and your vision. Don't leave the success of your students to chance. Fill every classroom with excellent educators by sharing your story and creating a magnetic force, no matter what it takes.

Messaging Your Priorities

The story you tell must clearly reinforce the school's vision and the major initiatives that are front and center for your team. Messaging clear priorities not only helps them to remain the focus of daily work but also defines the school itself, giving your school a unique identity that creates pride and ownership. If your school is focused on STEAM, for example, make sure that the story you tell consistently reinforces that focus so that the community and potential new hires are clear about your priorities, goals, and your means of achieving them.

That's precisely what people are searching for when they go looking for a new job, a place of pride and contribution. Data collected on the reasons that young leaders sought particular career paths and specific places of employment revealed that young workers, in particular, are looking for an "intellectual challenge" and an "opportunity to impact the world" (Coleman & Whitehurst, 2014). One might consider both of these answers to be inherent aspects in the role of educators, but, unfortunately, it's not always obvious within the system. Rather, the narrative is often about test scores and societal problems that overshadow the deep work being done daily that is transforming students' lives.

As a result, our message must be explicit about our purpose and our results. What we find with most social media posts regarding schools and districts is that the content is usually the "fun stuff." It's great to show the lighter, fun side of schools; in fact, it's important as you tell your story, but it's also of critical importance to create your brand by messaging your priorities so that you're attracting "followers" with like minds, ready to join the team when an opening arises. These priorities are always connected to the vision of the school and must be clear both internally and externally. When your vision directs your brand, you unlock the potential of a highly successful culture.

VISION + BRAND = CULTURE

Creating a school-wide vision might seem like basic practice these days, or at least it should be. With that said, getting everyone on the same page about the vision, really living it, is what sets great leaders apart from good ones. The vision of your school or district should be inspiring and action oriented, leading people into the future. Great vision statements and the best visionary leaders provide clarity, discipline, and consistency for the people within the organization (Sinek, 2009).

A clear school vision provides purpose for teachers, students, and the community; it's the determining factor for a positive culture. But, until recently, branding your school or district wasn't nearly as popular of a discussion as is the creation of vision statements and the need for positive school culture (Sinanis & Sanfelippo, 2015). Schools with powerful messages and strong brands realized early on that the school vision must take the form of branding in order to inform the public and demonstrate how the vision is being achieved.

A brand is typically associated with a product or business strategy, but the benefits of a school or district brand are becoming more widely accepted as important for telling your story (Sinanis & Sanfelippo, 2015; Whitaker, Zoul, & Casas, 2017). Schools can readily align their message with student achievement, school culture, and impact within the community, especially given all of the available technological platforms for developing and disseminating information.

The best part of branding is that it not only communicates a powerful message to your stakeholders but also attracts top talent. Talented people, top performers, are attracted to organizations that communicate a winning message, which makes branding that much more important for schools where the typical message has been one of dread or despair (Ravitch, 2010). In a time when district and school report cards are a federal requirement and are transparent for anyone to see, a recognizable and influential brand gives a school a competitive edge for hiring.

This is why branding must happen long before you're recruiting and scouting for talent. A solid hiring process is ongoing and cannot be dictated solely by vacancies. The mind-set shift is in thinking about hiring in the before, during, and after stages of an opening. The edge, here, is that your brand can attract talented people to your school even in times when vacancies aren't posted. Consider the Ron Clark Academy where the brand is one that screams both fun and success for anyone who wants to take up the challenge of working for Ron Clark, who has also communicated his high expectations for both students and staff. The brand attracts people from all over the world to visit the school; to learn from its policies, programs, and practices; and to work in a rigorous yet inspiring environment.

Some may argue that if every school communicated such fun and excitement as the Ron Clark Academy then the competitive edge wanes, diluting the power of school branding and decreasing the pool of available teachers. It is this type of scarcity philosophy that precisely restricts the profession. We argue that if every school was as exuberant as the Ron Clark Academy, then more people than ever would aspire to work in education.

The problem that education now faces is that high school and college students aren't choosing teaching as a career. One of the oldest and most noble professions on earth is no longer attractive since much of the joy found in teaching has succumbed to a fixation on results, policies, and overly burdensome regulations. Worse yet, this vicious cycle will continue since students within the K-12 system don't see teaching as a career filled with possibilities or a chance to make a difference but rather a job void of fun, excitement, and upward mobility.

If every school embraced the philosophy of the Ron Clark Academy, more students would see school as an incredible place to spend the rest of their lives, and more students would be applying to earn their teaching credential. This negative pattern is precisely why we're calling for vision and branding as a strategy to attract talent. A compelling vision coupled with a strong brand has the potential to overshadow negativity, creating a different narrative that attracts talent for the future of teaching.

The Vision Has to Match the Brand

The number one reason why most marketing strategies fail, according to the *New York Times* best-selling author and CEO of StoryBrand, Donald Miller (2017), is that they are too complicated for both the business and customers to understand. The same is typically true for vision statements in schools. They are too wordy and cumbersome and try to touch on too many points, losing both focus and inspiration.

Our tendency to use educational jargon alienates noneducators and creates grandiose statements that morph into run-on sentences, which may as well be better suited as insurance company clauses than vision statements. This is the primary reason why vision statements adorn the walls of our schools but yet no one—students, staff, or community—can articulate them when asked. One reason this happens is we haven't truly considered our brand, the aspects of schooling that we want to last a lifetime for our students.

In other words, we need to consider the greater impact that schooling desires to have on the life of a child. That's our brand, and like most businesses, if we complicate it too much, it will fail to communicate our message to the public or to potential employees. The vision of the school or district has to be parallel with the brand. The brand is what the school is set *to do*, while the vision is what the school desires *to become*. The key is that they match each another so that you're continually marketing your culture to the outside world to attract talented teachers for when a position becomes available.

It has long been understood that a strong vision "provides a sense of purpose for the organization and also for the individual members within it" (Whitaker, Whitaker, & Lumpa, 2009). We take this one step further to say that a truly strong vision is the nucleus of your brand, not only to provide motivation and purpose for the people within the community but also to provide motivation for anyone who may be looking for that same purpose for themselves as a teacher. But it's not just about clarifying the vision, owning it and branding it for the world; it must be alive and well established within the fabric of the culture of your school or district.

The Brand Has to Match the Culture

It doesn't matter if you lead a business, a nonprofit, a church, or a school; the brand of your organization has to match the culture within it. Denise LeeYohn (2018), author of *Fusion: How Integrating Brand and Culture Powers the World's Greatest Companies*, offers insight into why a culture–brand synthesis is required for optimal performance. "You build a great brand by operationalizing it—by using your brand purpose, values, and positioning to develop strategy and guide operations, so that your brand isn't just what you *say*, it's what you *do*" (LeeYohn, 2018).

This is a critical notion for schools where our communicated purpose is about supporting students and the communities from which they come by providing quality instruction, resources, and programs. This means that student learning must be at the center of every decision and must lead to results. Championing a brand is only as powerful as the outcomes it touts, and, unfortunately, due to a number of what Schmoker (2006) calls "buffers," which include a lack of supervisory practices, rewards for mediocrity, and burdensome yet ineffective school improvement documents, schools don't make the gains that they promise.

The good news is that schools with a strong vision and a brand to match it break the mold by getting everyone moving in the same direction. This must be true for all stakeholders—students, staff, and community. It's not a farce, and it doesn't have to be complicated. When everyone understands the vision, expects to be held accountable to operationalizing it daily, and knows how to achieve it given his or her role on the team, success is inevitable. That's also how schools and districts catch the eye of potential talent. Because the vision is clear, the brand is well known, and the culture within the system breaks through the buffers, featuring real gains for deserving students, the school's reputation is celebrated widely.

Once these principles are known and obvious on the outside, people will beat down the doors to get in. One of the first ways that culture–brand fusion takes hold, though, is in the setting of a few clear core values that drive the behaviors you desire from your teachers. Once these values take hold, they will become part of the identity of your school environment, attracting only people who want to behave in those same ways.

Chapter Focus Questions

1. Is your vision statement clear enough for anyone to understand and recite?
2. Is the culture of your school well communicated to the outside world?
3. Is your school brand the same on the inside as it is on the outside?

Chapter 2

Success Practices

Although cultural change is challenging and time-consuming, it is not only possible but necessary.

—Reeves (2009, p. 36)

CORE VALUES + ACTIONS = RESULTS

Knowing *what* to do and *why* to do it is often obvious. Unfortunately, doing the obvious is not always easy. Situations can appear to be straightforward and clear when they can quickly get twisted and muddy. However, organizations can protect themselves against this type of ambiguity by having clear core values, a set of defining characteristics. Take, for example, Merck, a global leader in medicines and vaccinations, which made a value-driven decision when it decided to manufacture Mectizan. Despite knowing that the cost of production and manufacturing would not yield a profit, Merck continued with Mectizan because of its principles.

Dr. Vagelos, former president and CEO, realized that Merck had the ability to cure river blindness, otherwise known as onchocerciasis, because it is caused by an infection from the parasitic worm *Onchocerca volvulus*. A terrible disease, predominant in third-world countries, river blindness afflicts the eyes with lesions and itching that can lead to blindness. The challenge that Merck faced, as described by Dr. Vagelos, is that the very people who needed the drug couldn't afford it. Despite the potential financial losses, and the burden that the company would shoulder, the final decision was to produce the medicine for anyone who needed it (Merck Offers Free Distribution of New River Blindness Drug, 1987).

17

As a company, Merck went back to its principles, which espouses the desire "to make a difference in the lives of people globally" and a mission that says "Save and improve the lives around the world." It simply couldn't stay true to its core value if it made decisions based only on the bottom line. From a business perspective, the decision was incredibly risky, maybe even financially irresponsible, yet Dr. Vagelos put people in need above profit. He couldn't *improve lives* and *make a difference* if his only true consideration was monetary gains.

Now, more than 40 years later, through the coordinated efforts of several value-guided organizations, 100 million people annually are protected from river blindness in 31 African countries (Francais, 2014). It is principle-based decisions like this one that earn Merck its status as one of the world's oldest yet largest pharmaceutical companies on the planet. Their reputation is what keeps them in business, and their values are what drive decisions regarding longevity, not money.

Successful organizations are grounded, as well as guided, by their core values, and this fact resonates throughout the community and builds a compelling reputation as a place that attracts people to be a part of the mission. These beliefs, which underpin the institution's vision, serve as powerful ideals to successfully navigate everyone's motivations, intentions, decision-making, and actions. Aligning the core values of the company with the actions of each person directly impacts the company's overall performance (Dilan, 2018). Each individual action affects every aspect of the organization, from the culture to the strategic implementation of a plan.

Schools are no different. They are dynamic systems with many moving parts and factors that contribute to student success. Clear, well-defined values embody the complexity of the system by harnessing the passion of each educator to drive decisions that are in the best interest of all children. These values provide "foundational commitments" so that educators are clear that each decision supports teaching and learning and that the school is heading in the right direction (Commission on Public Schools, 2016).

Familiar core values transcend all schools and represent the environment that most educators agree on for the sake of teaching and learning. Qualities like *respect, dignity, excellence,* and *integrity* are pillars for any educational organization. We often find them to be articulated as outcomes for students as they grow in an enriching, supportive, and safe atmosphere in schools. Another universal commitment is the unwavering belief among the school community that all students can learn. This value begins to transform a belief into action by taking outcomes for students into consideration through ownership. It's no longer about teaching and far more about learning.

This leads to what some schools are including in value statements—standards for adults and adult learning. Core values that consider teacher development ensure that the culture is about growth for everyone, not just our pupils. Well-developed values support the culture in a way that inspires action and results. They should make decisions easier, and they should create a reputation that withstands even the most difficult tests that present themselves, as in the story of Merck and the decision to put people over profits.

Our values in schools and districts give us prominence in the community and respect from afar so that when people think about the work of a teacher, they see it as dignified. When schools and districts have distinct values that create stature, they position themselves as an attractive place to work, which changes the game when we actually have an opening. Because not all schools communicate this way, using a set of defined core values, the ones who do have an advantage as they look to build their winning team. First and foremost, values that create a solid reputation are those that support both teachers and learners.

Values That Support Teaching and Learning

Educational core values are naturally student centered and for good reason, considering our primary purpose is to serve students. Children need to learn in the right environment, supported by all stakeholders and given equal access to the necessary resources. They need multiple opportunities to exercise and demonstrate what they've learned, and they need everyone to be on the same page about the support they require.

With that said, there are typically nonnegotiables regarding student achievement and instructional practices that come from the state or district office, putting pressure on teachers in the classroom (Marzano & Waters, 2009). Although some pressure is critical for student success, we also know the crippling effect that teacher turnover and teacher instability have on student learning. The pressure and support system are central to a value-driven organization because it creates a symbiotic culture of stress and encouragement, but this has to be equally balanced for teachers and students.

School systems that recognize and guide their actions based on the fundamental needs of students, as well as teachers, have an advantage. By creating supportive environments that sustain teacher development, they communicate a value for both the customer (students) and the staff (teachers). This value serves them through recruitment and retention efforts because when their reputation for providing supports exists within the community, they have interest in open positions long before the need to recruit.

One key method for creating a reputation that stands out as the desired place to work is to ensure that teachers benefit from a supportive environment with the right working conditions that actually motivate them to come back day after day. Quality resources, realistic class sizes, and adequate classroom conditions are key factors that demonstrate the core value that teachers matter as professionals (Johnson, Berg, & Donaldson, 2005).

The challenge is to create values that support students *and* teachers. And, although it may sound odd, supporting students and teachers through any given circumstance can create conflict for the decision-maker. This is where core values really act as a guide, which may push the decision-maker toward "what's best for students" but also, hopefully, keeping a consideration for a win-win. As Carroll, Fulton, Abercrombie, and Yoon (2004) describe, hiring qualified teachers is often not the issue; it's actually keeping them in these difficult situations. They leave because even the most basic needs for teaching and learning are not being met, including support from administrators as one of their top reasons (Carver-Thomas & Darling-Hammond, 2017).

We cover this aspect in greater detail in our book, *Retention for a Change*, when we dive into how we can motivate teachers by supporting and lifting them; however, the important part here (as we work to attract talent) is that the school develops a reputation that others want to experience. Schools that adopt clear values to support teachers demonstrate that the school community is willing to accept the responsibility to work beyond typical means to provide teachers with the necessary environment to be successful.

Schools with core values that support both students and teachers fully recognize the limitations of not doing so. When students are supported over the needs of teachers, staff stability suffers, creating a poor reputation as a place to work. When staff are supported over the needs of students, academic success suffers, creating an equally poor reputation as a place to teach. The key is a set of values that support both students and teachers as the beneficiaries of the brand, which is a vision and culture of excellence for everyone on the team. When values are clear, so are performance indicators, which provide clarity through an evaluation system that measures what matters.

Measuring Performance through a Value Lens

To make a meaningful difference in schools, core values must translate into action and action needs to be a consistent set of behaviors, a commitment to living out the desired results of the team (Whitaker, Zoul, & Casas, 2017). These value-driven actions need to be coupled with performance measurement systems that break down each aspect of the school and identify which areas are working and which areas are not. Regardless of the reasons, if there are areas that are not aligned to the core values of the school, then the leaders need to do everything possible to make each core value a reality by using other measures outside of the typical performance measurement system.

Each particular facet of the system that unifies to create a successful school must be continuously reviewed and measured for overall effectiveness. For example, we know that teacher satisfaction increases when teachers perceive their principal to be an effective administrator, one who provides support and who creates strong collegial structures (Blase and Blase, 2004). The evaluation must, then, point not at *what* is being done but rather *how* it is being done. The key to uncovering teacher satisfaction, in the case of administrator effectiveness, is in a keen understanding of how the administrator interacts with the staff and how the staff "feel" at work. Perceptions of support are impacted by the psychological aspects of working as much, if not more, as the actual work itself.

Similar in spirit to student and teacher evaluation systems, schools can adopt methods to determine the overall "health" of a school. Because we can practically enumerate much of what is needed within schools for teachers to be effective and for students to be successful learners, we can establish systems that measure how well we are supporting these efforts by taking a deeper look into the culture of a school and not just its practices.

Well-developed success measures, put in place to determine if the values are driving the work and whether the work is making the necessary gains, are the key to value-driven decision-making. The measurement outcomes provide data to support *how* things are going so that we can make adjustments to better support the people. When people feel supported, we create a reputation of responsiveness to their needs. Typical school measurement tools are about educational practices and miss the mark on the cultural significance of true success.

By staying true to our core values, we automatically align our actions with both our vision and what we want to accomplish within that vision. As so many systems of measurement have tried to accurately depict student achievement, we've missed the real nature of what *leads* to student achievement. When values are front and center with our actions aligned with them in our daily work, schools can thrive in a way whereby student achievement efforts almost fall into place. Of course, we account for the alignment between the written, taught, tested, and learned curriculum, as many of our colleagues have agreed is of critical importance. But even that won't matter if we aren't actively measuring the culture where the curriculum lives. Once the core values are clear and our actions are aligned, we can create a clear system to monitor progress. We revisit this concept of measuring culture in chapter 3 with our first technical tip.

MEASUREMENT + ALIGNMENT = OPTIMAL PERFORMANCE

The old adage "What gets measured gets done" is of particular importance for educational leaders who want their schools to actuate their vision and core values. Once school systems establish a clear vision and have agreed-on values, the real difficulty lies in making sure the words and statements actually drive the daily practices of the staff within the organization. This requires the challenging, but invaluable, process of weeding through all of the common day-to-day tasks to identify the critical, high-leverage best practices that fully represent the school's focus.

This level of clarity on what must be done on a daily basis positions the staff and the students to be successful. There are several powerful frameworks from which schools can model their key indicators, such as *The Education for Future Initiative*'s continuous improvement model (Bernhardt, 1999) or the *National Association of Secondary School Principals Breaking Ranks: The Comprehensive Framework for School Improvement* (National Association of Secondary School Principals, 2011).

Regardless of the chosen source, the key to sustainable success is in creating and tailoring a "site-specific model" that defines the daily "right work" and reflects the uniqueness of the school as well as its greatest needs (Marzano, Waters, & McNulty, 2005). We aptly name this "right work" with what we call "success practices" because they are the daily practices that lead to success. Once the *success practices* are selected, the next step in the process is to establish a clear methodology to assess the work being done and the culture in which the people do the work.

By accounting for alignment among the vision, the core values, and the daily success practices, the school is positioned to achieve its desired results. Again, we name the "right work" with the term "success practices" because there need to be a set of clear practices for success that everyone agrees are aligned with the vision and values. The final step is to determine a responsive way to measure progress, and, often, this means using multiple methods.

Many schools already have strategic plans that are clear and representative of the goals that the school wants to accomplish. However, a responsive assessment system further supports the plan by measuring the daily or weekly activities that are outlined in the plan and the culture in which the plan is executed. As for success practices, the significant difference is that this method of measurement is likened to using formative assessments versus summative assessments. The "low-stakes" data gathered formatively is designed to support and enhance practices, not judge and evaluate performance.

Although there is no magic formula for how often progress should be measured, the critical feature is that everyone is clear on how and when the school's performance is being assessed with all the data gathered and charted (Bernhardt, 1999). The measurement tool, as such, looks at the success practices within the culture as a representation of whether or not the behaviors of the adults match the vision and core values. In essence, we're measuring staff engagement with the work and the culture in which the work is being performed.

Consider one North American retailer that sought to increase the engagement of its 250,000-employee workforce. Its driving thought was that if it increased worker engagement the customer experience would improve as well. As a result, it partnered with a firm that helped it design and employ an online survey tool to continually reach workers, asking various questions regarding employee engagement and then giving the particular store managers the results. The task wasn't easy, the scope of this massive undertaking needed to be scaled, and gathering employee information also required a lot of trust from the employees.

Regardless of the complexities of the task, senior management understood that it had to connect with its workers, which meant hearing from them if they wanted to increase engagement and live out their core value of "engagement everyday" (Human Resource Executive, 2018). One of the important lessons learned for schools is that if administrators want to create an attractive and responsive work environment for their teachers, which reflects the core values and is committed to the daily success practices, a system must be in place to hear from staff on an ongoing basis.

This level of assessment has three powerful outcomes: (1) The information gathered is decentralized, which empowers people and creates trust. This empowerment increases ownership over what needs to be accomplished and infuses levels of responsibility and accountability within the culture of the school. And, by routinely assessing progress and evaluating what is and what is not working, leaders eliminate the once- or twice-a-year accountability "gotcha" report that is too often received negatively by the staff. (2) The information provides a granular approach to improvement. As Elmore and City (2007) write, achievement is not always obvious because we are looking in the wrong spots, such as annual achievement tests. By developing "finer-grained measures for improvement" school personnel are equipped to spot what's working and also make adjustments as needed to daily practice. (3) The assessments create the needed "mile markers" for celebration. As we wrote in *Passionate Leadership*, a key to positive culture is authentic celebration, and the best celebrations are a reflection of smaller goals met along the way to bigger ones (Thomas-EL, Jones, & Vari, 2020).

When measurement is aligned with actual practice and culture, the result is optimal performance. When people gain the self- and collective efficacy associated with a job well done, the school gains the reputation needed to attract more top talent. It's not just about performing well but also the reputation that we create when we do. The empowerment seeps through the walls of the school into the community and beyond.

Decentralizing Control by Empowering Everyone

The all-too-common command-and-control management style from a central hub doesn't leverage the level of sensitivity to the discrete particulars associated with student achievement. It should also be said that site-based control doesn't work either (DuFour & Marzano, 2011). Creating systems and processes for the various elements within an organization is a critical need for everything to function together harmoniously.

This happens when leaders use parameters that allow for creativity but without total mayhem or anarchy. In other words, we cannot control everything with policies, rules, and protocols, but we also cannot grant total freedom to do the work as anyone and everyone pleases. Establishing and maintaining organizational norms and clear expectations is a powerful way to guide the school without creating too many constraints.

However, once norms and expectations are established, school leaders must empower teachers to ensure that all facets of the complex school system are functioning optimally. This decentralization of control and empowerment recognizes that "under conditions of true complexity—where the knowledge required exceeds that of any individual and unpredictably reigns—efforts to dictate every step will fail. People need room to act and adapt. Yet they cannot succeed as isolated individuals, either—that is anarchy" (Gwande, 2009).

Schools have been fumbling with the same problems and issues for decades; one, in particular, is attracting and retaining quality teachers. A decentralized style of management accepts that there are persistent problems, and the key is managing them by creating strong teachers as leaders who can help solve problems. Too often, still, problems are centralized to small groups of people or individual leaders. It is only through webs of control and support that everyone is truly making an impact (Kotter, 2014).

Our symptomatic treatment of critical ailments will always fall short in the long term. As Gwande (2009) asserts, there are issues of "extreme complexity" that demand structures in place to offer support, which rely on everyone to be successful. Well-developed systems recognize that for proper execution to take place, the entire workforce must be on the same page (Harnish, 2014). In addition to measuring the day-to-day success practices, there must be a way to measure culture to ensure that core values are guiding the daily actions and how the people feel within the aligned system. What matters most to reputation is that the people within the organization have a feeling of purpose, empowerment, support, and care as they do the work. A decentralized system does more than empower the people closest to the work for optimal performance; it creates a symbiotic culture focused on both outcomes and people.

Assessments That Measure Effectiveness

Measuring the wrong thing is unfortunately all too common. In business, it may be a focus on revenue and not profit (Mauboussin, 2012). Too often, even as seen on *Shark Tank*, business owners report tons of sales but without real financial gains. In schools, this equates to an overreliance on student achievement data while ignoring or failing to collect critical teacher and community perception data. This type of data not only can yield powerful information from those on the front lines but also can send a clear message to teachers working in the school, and those seeking employment from the outside, that teachers are valued, their opinions matter, and they are an integral and influential part of the school.

Schools can take a page from the business book of management and identify the daily success practices as key performance indicators (KPIs). KPIs are defined in *MITSloan Management Review* by Schrage and Kiron (2018) as "the quantifiable measures an organization uses to determine how well it meets its declared operational and strategic goals." This will allow for continual feedback on those areas that matter most to teacher success and student achievement. Schools can adopt this common business strategy to ensure that the success practices are being used each day. This process should not be complicated. In fact, although it seems too simple, checklists have proven to be a powerful way to reproduce accuracy in diagnosing and treating complex situations. The recognized leader in developing and using checklists, The Flight Technical Safety group of Boeing, has influenced countless organizations.

> One of the most important beneficiaries of Boeing's checklist knowledge is the World Health Organization. Using ideas learned in part from Boorman and the Flight Technical & Safety team, a study of eight hospitals around the world showed that major complications for surgical patients decreased 36 percent after the introduction of checklists. Deaths fell by 47 percent. The World Health Organization now is creating and distributing checklists worldwide. (Brabant, 2010)

The brilliance behind checklists is the acknowledgment that simple reminders of what must be done are potentially overlooked due to basic human nature and the challenges and interruptions we commonly face during the daily grind of our work. Schools can harness the power of checklists by transforming their KPIs into simple "musts" that need to be done in each class period, every day, by every teacher or student. In chapter 3, we take a deeper dive into using KPIs in schools and then, by using our technical tip, you can assess your culture against the core values and success practices you've determined to be most important.

Chapter Focus Questions

1. Are your core values clearly defined as the critical behaviors that you expect in your school?
2. Do your core values support both teachers and students?
3. Are your success practices identified and measured on a regular basis?

Chapter 2

BUILDING A WINNING TEAM: THE MAGNETIC
REPUTATION MODEL

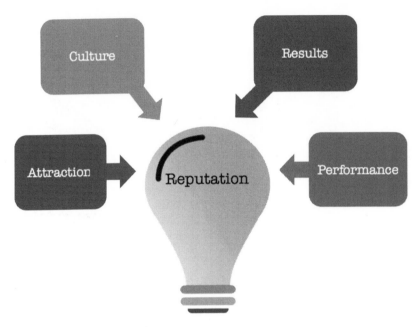

Figure 2.1.   The Magnetic Reputation Model
Source: **Courtesy of Joseph Jones.**

Chapter 3

Taking a Deeper Dive and Employing a Technical Tip

Culture

Without enough leaders, the vision, communication, and empowerment that are at the heart of transformation will simply not happen well enough or fast enough to satisfy our needs and expectations.

—Kotter (2012, p. 173)

In organizational design we often find dual-bottom-line systems that account for both the performance indicators of the company, typically calculated as profits, and the indicators of personal growth and professional fit for employees. Schools aren't generally equipped with the same outlook regarding the ability to assess both the daily success practices and the culture in which those practices are performed.

The following deeper dive takes a look into how KPIs can be used to employ and assess the implementation of success practices within a school setting, and the technical tip that follows demonstrates a way in which schools can assess six critical domains of culture, all of which are associated with support and better outcomes.

DEEPER DIVE 1: USING KEY PERFORMANCE INDICATORS TO EMPLOY SUCCESS PRACTICES

In order for the key performance indicators (KPIs) to be effective, enabling schools to reach their desired results, they need to be structured appropriately. The overall goal in the use of KPIs is to design a process that allows administrators to assess how well the school's core initiatives are making progress.

Furthermore, KPIs allow leaders to create checkpoints in time, rather than once or twice a year. To support and contribute to the overall effectiveness of the school, KPIs need a few critical features:

1. They need to be simple yet clear.
2. They need to represent the main priorities of the school.
3. They need to be supported with a manageable and user-friendly infrastructure that allows for the collection and analysis of data.

Schools cannot afford to create another burdensome task that frustrates the staff and doesn't produce results. A seamless KPI process provides administrators and teachers the needed time to spend reviewing and reflecting on the data to make informed decisions. With an established set of KPIs, schools can create simple checklists for review and evaluation of the success practices and their viability.

Consider our initial four arguments for creating a school that is grounded in developing a magnetic force to attract a loyal school community that is proud of its school. Telling your story and leveraging social media to inform the greater community can be filtered down into a few KPIs and then organized into a checklist that creates a thorough outlook of the ongoing important work. The performance indicator is "telling your story," while the success practices are anything that facilitates the story being told. The following is a sample checklist that organizes the primary methods in which a school can "tell its story" and inform the greater community of its accomplishments in a positive way.

KPI Checklist for *Telling Your Story*

KPI: Telling Your Story	*Responsibility*	*Audience*	*Frequency*
Newsletter	Administrative assistant	• Current families • Potential families • Legislators • Business community	Quarterly
Facebook posts	Student Social Media Club	School community	Daily
Twitter posts	Assistant principal	School community	Daily

This general checklist can be broken down further to ensure that every aspect is covered and completed with integrity. The following is a checklist for newsletters that guides the overall developers and helps them to make sure that all of the areas are met.

Newsletter	Component	Responsibility	Calendar/Due Dates
Fall newsletter	Important dates	Administrative assistants	End of August
	Message from the principal	Principal	Mid-September
	Important information	Assistant principal	Mid-September
	New staff	Administration	Mid-September
	Success stories 1. Academic 2. Extracurricular 3. Community 4. Alumni	1. Academic: department chairs 2. Extracurricular: athletic director 3. Community: assistant principal 4. Alumni: Booster Club president	Beginning of October
	Highlights/data	1. Attendance: secretary 2. School climate: counselors 3. Assessments: department chairs 4. Community engagement: assistant principal	Beginning of October
	Pictures	Student Social Media Club	Mid-October

To ensure the checklist is used and followed appropriately, it should be housed in an online shared document platform, such as Google Sheets. This allows for each person, who is responsible for a portion of the newsletter, to communicate his or her progress without having to meet face-to-face more frequently than necessary.

Consider a school's desire to create and implement higher-level questions used throughout every lesson. Often, a disparity between the level and type of questions being asked on an assessment and those asked in a classroom exists. To garner greater alignment, administrators rely on observations and walk-throughs to collect this type of data. By cataloging questions that are asked during lessons, administrators and a team of teacher leaders can determine how often deep questions are being employed with students. If deep questioning is a primary area of focus, among the school's *principles of instruction* (more to come in chapter 5), and is supported through professional development and professional learning communities (PLCs), teachers should use checklists to remind themselves while planning.

The checklist communicates the importance of planning the questions while at the same time collecting the actual questions being asked for review at a PLC, evaluating their strength, and confirming that the questions are grade-level appropriate. Typical classroom questions are too often not aligned with the grade-level assessments, and the checklist is a way to double down on making sure that deep questioning, as a KPI, is making its way into lesson plans on the frontend, versus the backend, during observations and walk-throughs. Student achievement is the ultimate goal, and when teachers are provided with an opportunity to perfect their craft through planning and reflection, we realize the goal faster. When our goals are met internally, it sends a clear message to anyone who wants to be part of a winning team.

KPI Checklist for *Deep Questioning*

Deep Questioning	*Question*	*Depth of Knowledge* *1, 2, 3, or 4*
Lesson planning: Did I preplan deep questionings?		
Lesson planning: Are the questions aligned with the essential question?		
Lesson planning: Are the questions able to help me know how well the students are learning the content?		

TECHNICAL TIP 1: THESCHOOLHOUSE302 REPUTABLE, EFFECTIVE, PERCEPTION SURVEY FOR SCHOOLS (REPSS)

TheSchoolHouse302 Reputable, Effective, Perception Survey for Schools (REPSS) is adapted from the Gallup survey items in *First, Break All the Rules* and from Gostick and Elton's *The Carrot Principle*. The survey analyzes six domains and uses a five-point Likert-style scale. The six domains of culture that we evaluate are *purpose, trust, accountability, support, growth,* and *innovation*. Each domain has 10 questions with a point value assigned to each one of the responses, totaling 50 possible points within each domain.

This approach gives you a quick insight into how you score within each area. This model represents the culture of what we consider a *reputable and effective school*. With a clear *purpose* guiding the team, *trust* among all team members, *accountability* for making a difference, *support* while working toward the goals, *growth* as an individual and as a team, and *innovation* as a core value, the culture of a reputable and effective school will assuredly attract top talent.

The survey provides a pulse on the culture of the school and how well it's functioning. Each domain represents a critical area of culture, and when schools achieve high scores within each domain, you can guarantee that the staff, the students, the families, and the community are going to be buzzing about your school and the success it is achieving. The key is for schools to work within these cultural domains for continuous improvement.

Growth and achievement are an ongoing process, and the survey can be administered at various times of the year to gather necessary data for informed decision-making. The use of the survey is flexible, and schools can decide what is most advantageous for them and their culture. We advocate using it as a pre- and post-assessment to gather critical data on the school year. Regardless of when it is administered, it is paramount that the team see the data and the survey as proactive measures to create the best possible school environment for everyone. The goal is for the entire staff to complete the survey, identifying only nominal demographic data, although you can add anything you wish to the model.

Finally, *TheSchoolHouse302 REPSS* is not designed to supplant any other principal evaluation tools, including student outcome data or principal evaluation systems. Instead, it's meant to supplement these tools by specifically measuring school culture, using the perceptions of the staff, so that we can reflect on levels of clarity, trust, accountability, support, growth, and innovation—all indicators of highly supportive and caring cultures.

Please take time to reflect on the following questions. Please use the following scale to record your answers.

A. Strongly Disagree   B. Disagree   C. Neutral   D. Agree   E. Strongly Agree

Each response has the following point value:

1   point for Strongly Disagree
2   points for Disagree
3   points for Neutral
4   points for Agree
5   points for Strongly Agree

Each section of the survey has 10 questions to equal 50 points. The higher the number, the more effective your school is in that particular area.

Purpose Questions   ***My Score*** ____/____

1. I know my purpose at work each day.
2. My purpose at work directly corresponds with my daily activities.
3. I feel connected to my work.
4. I see the results of my efforts.
5. I tell a positive story about my workplace.
6. The school brand communicated to the public is the same as the culture I experience as a professional.
7. Our school's core values are so clear that I know what is expected of me on a daily basis.
8. I find the work I do rewarding.
9. I'm inspired by the people with whom I work.
10. I am passionate about my daily purpose.

Trust Questions   ***My Score*** ____/____

1. I trust my coworkers.
2. I feel connected to my coworkers.
3. I can rely on my coworkers.
4. I trust my supervisor.
5. I can rely on my supervisor.
6. I trust my department head.
7. I can rely on my department head.
8. My colleagues treat me with respect.
9. The decisions made by administration are consistent with our core values.
10. The administration treats me with respect.

Accountability Questions   ***My Score*** ____/____

1. My supervisor holds everyone to the same level of accountability for the work.
2. My supervisor/administrator communicates clear goals for me.
3. My supervisor/administrator communicates measurable goals for me.
4. The principal communicates clear goals for the school.
5. The principal communicates measurable goals for the school.
6. I receive feedback on my performance each time I am observed formally.
7. I receive feedback on my performance each time I am observed informally (e.g., walk-throughs).

8. The feedback I receive includes specific praise (e.g., praise is aligned with our instructional focus).
9. The feedback I receive includes sufficient detail so that I can improve my performance (e.g., corrective feedback is clear about the adjustments I need to make to my instruction).
10. The feedback I receive helps me grow professionally.

Support Questions   My Score ____/____

1. Our school culture welcomes ideas and suggestions.
2. I feel comfortable going to my administration with issues.
3. My supervisor respects my suggestions and ideas.
4. The principal provides ample opportunity for suggestions and ideas regarding school initiatives.
5. I feel as if I'm on a team when I come to work.
6. I have been recognized recently for my contributions to the school.
7. My classroom is designed to help me do my job well.
8. My classroom is equipped with technology to facilitate student learning.
9. I have the necessary instructional materials to successfully meet the needs of all my students.
10. I feel supported by the administration.

Growth Questions   My Score ____/____

1. My supervisor encourages my learning and growth.
2. An administrator, other than my supervisor, has spoken to me this year about my progress as an educator.
3. There are opportunities to serve in leadership positions at my school.
4. The building-level professional learning I participated in this school year was relevant.
5. The building-level professional learning I participated in this school year was timely.
6. The building-level professional learning I participated in this school year was quality.
7. The district-level professional learning I participated in this school year was relevant.
8. The district-level professional learning I participated in this school year was timely.
9. The district-level professional learning I participated in this school year was quality.
10. I am given the opportunity to provide professional learning to my colleagues.

Innovation Questions   My Score ____/____

1. The staff at our school are made up of a diverse group of people.
2. My colleagues challenge my thinking in productive ways.
3. I am encouraged to take instructional risks in the classroom.
4. I use data to alter my methods of teaching to improve student achievement.
5. I used what I learned in professional development this year.
6. I was recognized for being innovative with our practices.
7. Overall, innovation is a norm at our school.
8. I feel comfortable expressing new ideas to my colleagues.
9. I feel comfortable expressing new ideas to my administration.
10. Our school has a method for me to express new or different ideas.

THE CULTURE IS FOR THE PEOPLE WHO ARE DOING THE WORK

You build a culture to support the people doing the work. The reputation of your school is not merely the creation of an outward-facing advertisement of something that isn't validated by the people on the inside of the organization. The opposite is true. The people doing the work *are* the culture; the culture is made *by* them, *for* them. What we know is that the story of your culture will get told. That story is either told *by* you or told *about* you.

Great organizations learn to tell their story in such a compelling way that it creates an attraction. When outsiders find your school's story to be appealing to what they consider to be a reputable brand, they seek you (and not the other way around). When you finally have talent beating down the doors of your school, your selection team can be picky about putting together a team of elite players.

When core values are put together with real action, the result is always success. When KPIs are aligned with success practices that get measured to determine effectiveness, we can transcend systems of accountability. Only then will the people be empowered within the culture to make the difference that they intended to make when they joined the team.

Too many systems are mired in the muck of creating a culture *around* the people, and they miss the need for the people to be the drivers of the culture so that the momentum of the school creates its own allure. We have always said that school systems must have accountability from within, and the pressures from the outside simply won't make the needed changes that can come only from the candor and compassion that we experience with one another (Jones & Vari, 2019). And, when the culture speaks for itself, we get to define, more than ever before, the beliefs and behaviors that support the culture along with how we expect the people to communicate and work within it.

Chapter Focus Questions

1. How can you employ KPIs to track progress with one of your key success practices?
2. How do you currently measure culture to ensure that your team is creating a positive reputation for itself?
3. How and when might you adapt or adopt a survey like *REPSS*?

Chapter 4

Attracting Elite Talent

Soft skills catch our eye because they are beautiful: Picture the soccer star Lionel Messi improvising his way to a brilliant goal, or Jimi Hendrix blazing through a guitar solo, or Jon Stewart riffing through a comic monologue. These talents appear utterly magical and unique.

—Coyle (2012, p. 24)

PRACTITIONER SPOTLIGHT

When Robert Kinghorn arrived at Wasatch Elementary School, the teacher turnover rate and staff morale were growing concerns. And, when positions became available, it was difficult to get applicants because of what Robert describes as "a false perception of the school and its community." In two years, the team turned it around completely by changing the culture from the inside out.

Robert even told us a story about a teacher who moved away and then came back, all because of the school culture that his team created. He talked about people taking positions in his school that they didn't otherwise see themselves doing just so that they could join the team, in hopes of finding their niche. He referenced hiring people for who they are and not a set of skills they bring. Everything he told us was about the character of the people doing the work and the difference that they wanted to make in the lives of young people.

These days, Robert tells a different story about teacher turnover. He still loses more teachers than he would like but all to new leadership positions. Because Wasatch has practically become a leadership development site, his teachers move on to teacher trainer positions and district-level mentoring

roles. Instead of a culture where staff are broken down to the point of res-
ignation, or trying to find "greener pastures," they are built up to a point of
promotion.

The number one reason that Robert sites as the attraction and retention
point is *culture*. It's the culture that attracts top talent. He built a winning
team, and now everyone who hears about it wants to belong to this awesome
culture, which is palpable from the moment you enter the doors at Wasatch
Elementary School. You can learn more from Robert Kinghorn by following
him on Twitter @rwkinghorn.

THE ARCHETYPE OF A TEACHER

Beliefs and behaviors are the map of a person's soul. The beliefs and behaviors of a staff profoundly impact the culture of a school as employees' actions
help construct and contribute to the overall work environment. The pressing
question for any school is whether the individuals who comprise the staff are
a positive or negative force. There are archetypes of the staff members who
can make or break your culture, and your culture is what speaks to the community, determining your reputation.

The first step in attracting elite talent to your school is in knowing precisely
which qualities and characteristics you desire in an employee. By creating a
talent archetype of the kind of people who work (or whom you want to work)
in your department, school, or district, you set a standard of excellence. Seth
Godin's famous ideas about marketing reveal that building your brand is
about a story for the audience you wish to reach. The talent archetype identifies the characters whom you want to be in your story and who will build and
support the reputation you desire.

For this desire to come to fruition, our product (in this case our school)
must be supported by a tribe, a group of committed and unwavering individuals with a clear purpose and a sense of responsibility to something larger than
themselves. These individuals feel a sense of belonging, as in "people like us
do things like this" (Godin, 2018). The power in this statement comes from
our ability to define the "us" and the "this."

When school leaders clearly identify which attributes are most important
for their people to have, they are far more likely to attract those attributes to the
team. A reputable brand attracts quality candidates and clearly distinguishes
the traits that make for an elite performer from those who are mediocre. The
good news is that creating your archetype doesn't have to be complicated.
Take, for example, Graber's (2015) employee "engagement archetypes." The
"all star" is the quintessential engaged employee who possesses the combination of the traits "constructive" and "positive." This individual is completely

different from the "saboteur" who epitomizes toxicity. By clearly identifying the archetypes of what employee engagement looks like, Graber provides clarity and insight regarding employee commitment.

Within education, we can also identify and create the prototypical teacher we need in the classroom versus those individuals whom we don't. If we want *all star* players on the team, they must possess the attitudinal characteristics of a positive performer and the constructive characteristics of someone who looks for ways to improve himself or herself and others. This might mean that the archetype of the exemplar teacher we are looking for includes only people who are confident, expressive, positive, hardworking, and value driven. Now we have a five-point model of our archetype that represents the qualities of the professionals within the organization.

In turn, this will directly impact the culture of the school, sending shock waves throughout the community, which then communicates the reputation we desire for our school and the people working in it. This includes the students as well, and when the staff model these behaviors, the students will learn them.

Great leaders also recognize the sensitive relationship between high-achieving, passionate employees and a positive and rewarding culture. If the culture is disempowering, your greatest and most valuable employees are the first to be affected. Two important factors must be accounted for: (1) The most passionate people are also the most marketable, and (2) the most passionate people also tend to be the most sensitive in the group (Gostick & Elton, 2007). This means that leaders must take heed to the fact that the best people are always being recruited by other organizations.

Top talent, those needed to build, shape, and sustain the organization's reputation, can easily be the first to go to another school based on their brand. Top-tier talented people are creative and fun, meaning they need space to expend their energy and an environment that supports their growth. If the organization doesn't support and fuel them, then they'll leave. "People might join a company for the compensation, growth opportunities, or mission, but they frequently leave because they don't have a good relationship with their manager" (Altman, 2017). Attracting top talent by identifying the archetype is critical, but keeping high performers and building a winning team that, in turn, has the reputation to attract more talent rest solely on leadership.

Learning from the Laws

In his epic book, *The 21 Irrefutable Laws of Leadership*, John Maxwell introduces readers to the law of magnetism, which states that "who you attract is not determined by what you want. It's determined by who you are" (Maxwell, 1998). This is a critical notion for leaders who desire to build a winning team because your archetype will become a reality only when it goes beyond a simple list of key traits for *employees*.

The list must also develop into the critical characteristics that you desire to experience within *yourself*, exemplified through your actions as the leader. To attract the archetype you desire, you must exhibit the qualities you want. And because leadership is predominantly an outward magnification of oneself, the reality is that it's mostly through self-development and internal exploration that we yield our greatest growth.

> I believe that leaders at every level and in every position have an intrinsic responsibility to question who they are being while they are leading. But it takes a committed leader to embrace the search for truth as a criterion for leadership, and not everyone can achieve this. Very few are willing to embark on an inner journey to discover what propels them. (Daskal, 2017)

Great leaders are never flawless, perfect, or all knowing. In fact, all leaders have weaknesses and gaps. Oddly, the same qualities that make them great can also be a potential liability, which creates "competing sides, a polarity of character" within them (Daskal, 2017). Understanding this dynamic is a primary reason why the archetype you create is so important. It serves as a reminder of who you want to be and the quality of the individuals you want to attract.

Interestingly, though, this concept of magnetism also has its own polarity, which can trap our thinking if we're not attentive to it. We must be mindful of the one magnetism pitfall, especially when hiring. As we embrace the law of magnetism, we must also be deliberate not to narrow our view of who we are looking to attract in terms of a well-rounded team. The archetype represents the ideal characteristics that best serve the needs of the students and the school. As long as that remains the backdrop behind whom we are looking to hire, we maintain an openness to all candidates and their unique talents that they bring, which will best serve the school community.

But take pause. When magnetism is at its best, you must "work at recruiting people who are different from you to staff your weaknesses" (Maxwell, 1998). Knowing what your students and school require to be successful, along with having a keen insight into your own strengths and weaknesses, is the key to attracting the best candidates and rounding out your team. The archetype is about character, and it cannot overshadow diversity.

Value Diversity and Diversity Will Be of Value

A key to your winning team is diversity. For the team to be successful, for the players to reach all students, and for its reputation to universally attract top talent, the staff members must come from various backgrounds with demographic differences. In addition, considering the complexities of the needs of students and the challenges associated with teaching them, school leaders must understand that diversity goes beyond the traditional definition.

As you develop a team with the predefined archetypal characteristics, you also need the staff to possess both "cognitive diversity" (Reynolds & Lewis, 2017) and "2-D diversity" (Hewlett, Marshall, & Sherbin, 2013) so that you can create a thriving academic culture. "Cognitive diversity has been defined as differences in perspective or information processing styles. It is not predicted by factors such as gender, ethnicity, or age" (Reynolds & Lewis, 2017). The greatest outcome of a cognitively diverse team is that they solve problems faster than a nondiverse group of thinkers.

In a study of executive leaders, the diversity actually "accelerated learning and performance in the face of new, uncertain, and complex situations" (Reynolds & Lewis, 2017). Consider the implications within a PLC (professional learning community) conversation around what to do when students don't understand or what to do when they do understand (DuFour & Marzano, 2011). Cognitive diversity can lead to improved lesson planning, innovative approaches to remediation and enrichment, and stronger student outcomes, making it a leadership imperative for school success and a reputable system. The second type of diversity is 2-D diversity, which consists of *inherent* and *acquired* diverse traits.

> Inherent diversity involves traits you are born with, such as gender, ethnicity, and sexual orientation. Acquired diversity involves traits you gain from experience: Working in another country can help you appreciate cultural differences, for example, while selling to female consumers can give you gender smarts. We refer to companies whose leaders exhibit at least three inherent and three acquired diversity traits as having two-dimensional diversity. (Hewlett, Marshall, & Sherbin, 2013)

Two-dimensional diversity among school personnel has numerous benefits and deserves a book all to itself. Schools are generally sensitive to the inherent diversities among their staff when developing their team, but there is incredible value in identifying the necessary acquired diversity that could truly benefit students and the organization as a whole. That said, some of the obvious student benefits are stronger connections among the school, students, and their families; an increased awareness and appreciation of the differences among the student body; and an ongoing awareness of the depth of communication necessary to elicit partnerships.

Regarding the organization, there exist the potential for greater synergy among the faculty, an understanding of the power behind ongoing feedback and sharing ideas, and an appreciation for the talents each individual brings to the organization. Schools that value this level of diversity benefit from it immensely, and the number one beneficiaries are the students. Finally, when teachers and support staff come from diverse backgrounds, you create a reputation in the community that you're in search of diverse thinkers, diverse people, and diverse experiences. Only then will diversity beget more diversity in the people who apply for your jobs when they're posted.

LEADERSHIP TEAM ACTIVITY 1: DEVELOPING THE ARCHETYPE OF A TEACHER

This activity is intended to take place at a leadership team meeting. We make the assumption that most schools, small and large, operate with a team of teacher leaders at the helm. With everything that gets heaped on school principals, the job is practically impossible without a team of teacher leaders to help with everything from management to instructional leadership to decision-making (DuFour & Marzano, 2011; Fullan, 2014).

The best school leaders know how to strike the balance between delegating and ownership, and the key to this rests in the time spent on professional development for teacher leaders. Whether or not leadership teams meet weekly or twice per month, the number of meetings is only as valuable as the content and productivity of the meeting. Too often, the "stuff" of the meeting is about the minutiae and practical aspects of a school—schedules, curriculum work, assessment calendars—and, although important, there is not enough time dedicated to learning and growing as teachers and, more specifically, as teacher leaders.

Simply put, more time needs to be spent on capacity building and developing leadership skills associated with organizational development that extend beyond just classroom expertise. The good news is that leadership team meetings are a great place to start because the team is together in one place with the time reserved for doing the work. "The deepest learning for team leaders occurs when they learn by doing—when they are engaged in real work in the context of their own school" (DuFour & Marzano, 2011).

Open the meeting by saying that you want to define the ideal teacher. These are qualities that you and the team feel are important to determine the reputation of your school and the people who work in it. Stay away from hard skills, like classroom management or content knowledge. Stick with soft skills and personality traits similar to what was previously identified—confident, expressive, positive, hardworking, and value driven—ensuring that the specific attributes are important to the teaching profession and unique to your school because of the community it serves.

The good news is that many of the skills that teachers need to have in their role are available and discussed in the literature on teaching. In fact, whole evaluation systems are based on these qualities. The bad news is that drawing on the literature to support the ideal archetype of a teacher yields scarce resources. Rather than skills, we're talking about virtues and character traits. Many teacher contracts have morality clauses, but that is not what we are referring to in this regard. We are looking to identify the characteristics that most support the qualities and virtues that comprise an ideal master teacher.

What is often attributed to a teacher are the observable and technical skills, and very little has been said about personality or character in the classroom. In one study, though, conducted by Pearson, five true qualities emerged, including the ability to develop relationships, kindness, patience, and dedication (Peterson-DeLuca, 2016). Even so, that study identified skills as well, such as an understanding of students' developmental levels and cognitive, emotional, and behavioral engagement. Entire teacher preparatory college coursework is dedicated to these but nothing, necessarily, to the nature of a positive attitude. However, we contend that, as we continue to move in the direction to support students in responsive ways through restorative practices and such, these characteristics are critical.

Dedicate ample time for the team to identify their list of characteristics, and push them to define what each of them means for the school. In our book *Passionate Leadership: Creating a Culture of Success in Every School* (2020), we defined "passion" in schools as being three things: a desire to grow, a strong work ethic, and an incredibly positive attitude. In the case that the team selects "passionate" as one of the qualities for your archetype, push them to say what that means.

Archetype Quality	What It Looks Like
Passionate educator	Willingly takes instructional risks for the betterment of students
	Builds relationships with parents and the community
	Enthusiastically participates in PLCs
	Embodies the four Cs:
	• Crazy about kids
	• Curious about their lives
	• Consistently leads
	• Creates a culture of love

Allow the team to grapple with this concept of an archetype, but land on four to eight qualities, each with its own definition. To aid them in this task, ask them direct and explicit situational questions that prompt their thinking and personalize the process. Consider the following questions:

- What does a passionate educator's daily lesson look like?
- How does a passionate educator contribute to our PLC?
- How does a passionate educator conduct himself or herself in our professional development?

- How does a passionate educator interact with students?
- What would a phone call home sound like from a teacher driven by passion?
- What is his or her attitude toward difficult circumstances and change?

Once the list is clear, you have your portrait, and when everyone understands the beliefs and behaviors that are most important to the school, we can work to begin to hold one another accountable to them, creating a reputation that we want the school to have. With the right reputation, you'll never be in a pinch when hiring season comes around.

Waiting to define what we need, in general, when a vacancy occurs, is too late and too often simply a reaction to the void rather than preparing for it ahead of time. Of course, having an archetype doesn't mean that everyone is a clone and that all your hiring issues are solved. Just the opposite is true. When we define the attitudinal and social characteristics of our desired workforce, we allow for every other aspect of a diverse staff to thrive.

Leadership Team Guiding Questions

1. What are the personality traits most important to our team?
2. How do we define each of these characteristics?
3. What do they look like in action?

Chapter 5

Performance, Passion, and Professional Learning

The best make everyone around them better.

—Gordon (2009, p. 148)

PRACTITIONER SPOTLIGHT

Brendalyn King shared with us a dynamic story about building a school's reputation from inception to exception. She and another cofounder started Leadership Prep Ocean Hill Charter School (LPOH), an Uncommon Schools charter, in Brooklyn, New York, in 2010, and by 2017, the school was a National Blue Ribbon winner. With a population of 99 percent minority and 82 percent economically disadvantaged, the school services its surrounding community, which has one of the highest poverty rates in the country. Despite their circumstance and uphill battle, Brendalyn describes an award-winning culture that attracted staff due to their crystal clear vision and core values.

LPOH was fortunate to have a parent organization, Uncommon Schools, that helps with community engagement and enrollment, but Brendalyn and her team couldn't rely on that alone to build their reputation. It required an unrelenting desire and unconventional ways to bring the school to success. To realize their vision, it took sweat and tears, along with extremely long days and nights, planning and strategizing how to attract high-quality teachers to support the incoming low-performing students.

King says that to garner the community's ear, she attended council meetings, stood in subway entrances, provided information at community centers, and went to local churches every week. The school's continued success is attributed to a culture that centers on learning and love. A true tribute to building a winning team through a reputation of success, LPOH and cofounder

45

Brendalyn King are a spotlight of achievement that started with telling their story in a way that created their positive momentum. You can learn more from Brendalyn King by following her on Twitter @BrendalynK.

CREATING OPTIMAL PERFORMANCE

Leveraging the unique talents and diversity that comprise your team creates situations that require people to rely on one another. People thrive in situations where "partnerships harvest the potential of the team" (Blanchard & Muchnick, 2003). Respecting the diversity of each person also requires teachers to work and learn in a responsive system, which allows each individual to grow because of the supportive nature of the environment. It's within this type of culture that teachers develop into masters.

To create scenarios for optimal performance, schools must instill a never-stop-growing mentality among their staff. Interestingly, most educators are fully aware of the power of self-efficacy and "grit" for students, including the impact it has on academic success. Schools have embraced the pioneering work of Bandura (1995), Dweck (2008), and Duckworth (2016), as well as others, to equip the staff with particular skills needed to work with students to help them navigate toward success as learners. As such, much of student achievement hinges on their own perception of their aptitude and ability (Hattie, 2009), and schools have adopted many practices outside of the traditional educational realm of curriculum and instruction to increase opportunities to learn using the exploration of one's beliefs through metacognitive practices (Wilson & Conyers, 2016) and lessons that reach toward self-actualization (Smith, Chavez, & Seaman, 2017).

This ongoing focus, however, remains mostly concentrated on the students; we contend that schools must now pivot this attention to mind-set work for the adults as well. The impact of these transformative practices will be a complete redesign in the way that adults interact with one another and with students. And, ultimately, this work should guide how administrators approach the growth and development of their instructional staff.

One of the most common phrases used in education is "professional development." School systems are committed to and invested in teacher development, reportedly to the tune of $18 billion annually (Education Next, 2018). However, reports demonstrate that these professional development efforts fall short of producing real change (Darling-Hammond, Hyler, & Gardner, 2017), and they are not improving teacher performance unless done correctly. To attack this problem, only one primary solution emerges: teachers need a more active role in their learning.

Much like the efforts to engage students, putting them in a position to own their learning through choice, particularly their learning goals (Anderson,

2016), administrators can turn the corner as well by empowering staff to take ownership of their own growth. As efforts are being made throughout school systems to revisit what it means to be an actively engaged student through empowerment and experiential scenarios, administrators must also "let go" and turn over the professional learning to the staff.

Too often, PD is not even viewed as real *p*rofessional *d*evelopment but rather a *p*rescription for *d*isaster. It is delivered in the precise fashion that we abhor when we see it done in the classroom, the sage-on-the-stage, sit-and-get style, delivery of content. Turning over the learning to the teachers, having them set personal growth goals that are aligned with the vision of the school, empowers them and respects the diversity and uniqueness that resonate through the teaching ranks, delivering a clear message of professionalism that appeals to top talent. Schools that empower teachers to be the owner of their learning experiences build a reputation that speaks to educators far and wide. This creates a different type of marketing strategy when positions become available to join for a staff who is engaged like this.

Many educators grumble about the overreliance of standardized assessments to determine student achievement. The one-and-done academic data snapshots are denounced as invalid indicators of student learning, yet administrators fall prey to the same trappings of efficiency, using policies over quality practices and core values. As intermittent teacher evaluations remain the crux of evaluating performance, despite their limited scope, teacher growth is simply limited. Worse yet, great teachers and experienced ones often receive the least attention, with little feedback and support to get better.

To remedy this problem of infrequent classroom visits, walk-throughs emerged with the intent of providing administrators with shorter but more frequent snapshots of what is occurring in the classroom (Downey, Steffy, English, Frase, & Poston, 2004). Performed correctly and collectively, evaluations and walk-throughs can provide administrators insight into how well a classroom teacher is performing. However, having insight into a teacher's performance does not translate into teacher growth. We are not suggesting that practice is either bad or ineffective. We do suggest an uptick in the candor we use when we discuss the improvements to practice that need to be made for stronger student outcomes (Jones & Vari, 2019). But, rather, we are calling for a revolution for how teachers are empowered and what actually leads to professional growth.

We liken this to one of our favorite famous quotes, often attributed to Einstein: "The definition of insanity is doing the same thing over and over again and expecting a different result." The challenge with using the teacher evaluation system and walk-through practices for professional development is that both are administrator-driven tasks. Continuing to do both without another value-added strategy to empower teachers will only yield the results that we've seen to date regarding professional learning.

Neither walk-throughs nor evaluations are void of the teacher, but that doesn't mean that the teacher is necessarily engaged. The need exists for a complementary activity that puts the teachers in a position to own their development. We expect teachers to create learning environments for students to increase self-motivation, active engagement, and more learner self-direction. We do this because these qualities better position students to learn, but these strategies are not limited to the adolescent brain.

Adult learners require the same conditions to truly impact their growth, leading to change and development. Administrators can create an environment in schools where teacher-directed personal development allows them to reflect and grow, using their experiences as a guide. A supportive growth-oriented culture is exactly what talented teachers are looking for when they decide to leave their stale and stagnant current roles, and it's precisely what our current preservice teachers are looking for in their first setting as an educator.

The overreliance on administrative-driven performance feedback ultimately limits the potential of teacher growth. "Findings show that individuals who are given time to articulate and codify their experience with a task improve their performance significantly more than those who are given the same amount of time to accumulate additional experience with the task" (Di Stefano, Gino, Pisano, & Staats, 2014). Assuming that teachers will grow simply through their experiences as teachers and by offering periodic professional development is unreasonable.

Performance evaluations and walk-throughs are critical tools for any instructional leader, but when used alone, they will not be transformative. The key to teacher development and a reputation for empowering staff is in the integration of a predefined set of instructional practices with individual and group reflection. The outcomes go well beyond the classroom, and talented teachers are dying to find a school that supports them in this way.

The Actuation of an Instructional Model

Having clear *Principles of Instruction* as a school is critical to supporting teachers' use of high-leverage strategies that offer students the greatest opportunity to learn. Schools commonly adopt instructional models or key strategies to guide teaching practices and create professional development opportunities, which support the proper understanding and use of each strategy. We take this two steps further to say that (1) the instructional model should be a set of "principles" that all teachers use for planning and preparing lessons, every lesson, every day, *and* that (2) one to four of the principles should be set as an "instructional focus" for the school year (or a preselected time frame) for reflection and learning.

The potential power for teacher development lies at the intersection between enumerating the teaching strategies themselves (*Principles of*

Instruction) and prompting teachers to actively reflect on their experiences using the strategies. The reflection should include both the teacher's perspective as a lesson planner and how well the students grasped the information because of the use of a given strategy.

Having *Principles of Instruction* as a school-wide success practice provides clarity for teachers in terms of planning and in terms of what supervisors are looking for when they visit classrooms for observations and walk-throughs. *Principles of Instruction* can be adopted from any number of research-based lists of instructional practices published by Hattie (2009), Marzano, Pickering, and Pollock (2001), Lemov (2015), or others who have published tips and techniques for engaging students for the sake of learning.

The key here is that the strategies create a sense of security and clarity for teachers because not only are they privy to the research on what works best for student learning, but they get psychological safety in knowing the expectations for performance. All three—the *principles* themselves, the safety they create, and the performance optimization—spawn the reputation that great schools boast as industry leaders in creating student success.

As for a clear instructional focus, if a school adopts only a few key strategies from the *principles* for the year, the goal should be that teachers become masters at executing the strategies. The mastery experience ties directly into one's self-efficacy, "the belief in one's capabilities to organize and execute the courses of action required to manage prospective situations" (Bandura, 1995), and further supports both the feeling of safety and optimal performance.

Winning teams have clear and specific ways in which people are expected to work along with supports to improve practice. When performance indicators and success practices are not clear, it's also not possible to improve our practice, at least not at any significant rate. It's also important, from the standpoint of building a reputation of success and safety, that providing lists of strategies is in no way a limit on the teachers' freedom to plan. In fact, it's liberating.

The safety comes from knowing the expectation with the strategies, while the freedom remains with the activities that teachers prepare to meet the demands of having to plan using the *Principles of Instruction*. The outcome in actuating *principles* goes beyond the school environment because as teachers learn to plan in similar ways with similar structures, the traditional isolated approach to planning is broken down, creating comradery and friendships beyond the working experience.

Positive Outcomes

Professional learning communities (PLCs), structured around success practices, to include *Principles of Instruction* (from the previous section), are the optimal place for not only reflecting on student performance but also increasing teacher expertise. Research reveals that there is significant gains in perspective and performance when using the power of continuous reflection through a cycle of inquiry, including "collaboration, mutual accountability, knowledge sharing, hub support, and feedback" (Learning Forward, n.d.).

This cycle is the key to continued and profound student improvement (DuFour & Marzano, 2011). The laser focus on student growth not only yields greater student achievement because students are making gains but also improves teaching through reflection and development. The PLC is the hub where teachers grow as a result of their discussions about student learning. This process of teacher development should be explicit, though, and used to build the individual as well as the team.

It eliminates any potential isolation, spurred from individualized planning time or a lack of inquiry about strategies (common *Principles of Instruction*), activities (plans for engaging students in the work), and student learning outcomes (data from formative and summative assessments). People want to work in a supportive environment where vulnerability is accepted as a norm. It's important for organizational design that people be honest about their experiences and their challenges, with continual improvement as the end goal. The cycle of inquiry used in a PLC is powerful, and its strength lies within the team's ability to continually reflect on student learning and their own performance.

As the cycle continues, the strength of the team grows within its collective self-awareness and ability to identify what's working and what isn't (Goleman, Boyatzis, & McKee, 2002). The positivity that results from successful team dynamics creates trust, support, faith, passion, and love. The outcomes of a great team are clearly demonstrated through care, connectedness, and commitment to one another (Gordon, 2018).

When this happens, relationships extend beyond the workday into the evenings and weekends. Friendships are formed. The true power of a positive culture creates the reputation that the school is more than a school; it's a tribe of people who care so deeply for one another and the work that their bond best not be disturbed by an "outsider," unless, of course, that outsider wants to join the team. That's how the strength of your reputation attracts even more top talent to your school and district.

LEADERSHIP TEAM ACTIVITY 2: SUPPORTING THE WORK THROUGH A CLOSED-LOOP COMMUNICATION SYSTEM

This activity is intended to support PLCs by providing a clear process and methodology to foster effective collaboration among group members to enhance their performance. Previously, we mentioned the power in having schools identify key performance indicators (KPIs) to ensure alignment between predetermined success practices and the actual work being done within classrooms and throughout the school.

We then couple KPIs with the proven accountability found within check-lists, used for the sole purpose of making sure that everyone is completing the identified work in time. The next step brings all of these efforts together by finding the time and the space to reflect on the practices, analyze them, and assess the outcomes. This is particularly useful in determining whether the agreed-on *Principles of Instruction* and the corresponding activities that teachers are actually using in their classrooms are making a difference for student achievement and their own professional growth.

PLCs are a powerful way to focus on student learning and refine teacher expertise. The challenge is to confirm that PLCs are functioning on a high level through proven methods of facilitation for maximum effectiveness. DuFour (2004) clearly identifies the needed structures that must be in place to support student learning and teacher growth within the PLC setting. Teaching and learning is at the heart of PLCs, and the key ingredient is effective, data-driven, result-oriented collaboration.

This level of collaboration goes beyond the traditional focus of students and hones in on teacher performance through discussions, reflection, and feedback. One goal of a strong PLC is to review how well the instructional focus of the school is being exercised within the classroom. This is where the three key areas of collaboration, learning, and results merge together for alignment and improved teacher performance. These three areas—collaboration, learning, and results—must always be connected to the school's professional development efforts, which are supported in PLCs.

It's within the PLC that teachers have the opportunity to reflect on their execution of a strategy to determine how effective their own practices are, including how well they are actuating the instructional focus. The PLC focus model demonstrates the relationship that the focus has to professional development and the PLC.

PLC FOCUS MODEL

Note that the focus strategy is at the center of the circle. Using the strategy as an instructional practice is professional development, especially if it's new or newly used, but the bigger deal for teacher growth is discussing the use of the strategy in a PLC, reflecting aloud and collaborating with others. Collaboration is a growing practice within schools as we further realize that silos and isolation are detrimental to teacher improvement.

Figure 5.1.   PLC Focus Model
Source: **Courtesy of Joseph Jones.**

However, as schools build better methods to focus on student learning outcomes, teacher expertise and growth tend to fall into the penumbras. When
data garners too much of the attention, actual practice gets overshadowed.
The collaboration on assessment reports is always important, but the conversations within the PLC must eventually pivot to the teachers' techniques,
how well they execute, what obstacles they face, and what adjustments need
to be made to instruction. This type of environment demands authenticity
and candor for meaningful dialogue among group members, which requires
trust—trust in both the process and the people.

To build this level of trust and commitment to growth for students and
teachers, schools can adopt a simple management method and meeting structure. A "closed-loop communication system" simply identifies critical information for sharing and reinforces the reflection process through necessary

feedback (Peyre, 2014). The way it works is that everyone comes to the table with something to share, and everyone else comments on it with either a probing question or something further to add. Closing the loop means that no one shares without getting feedback on what he or she said.

In other professions, such as health care, this type of team communication loop reduces efficiency errors in both time and execution (Peyre, 2014). To use a closed loop in PLCs means identifying a key strategy to discuss, reflecting out loud how you felt it went in the classroom, and then hearing from all of your PLC partners based on your comments. Each person takes a turn, and everyone gives and gets feedback. Let's take a look at a simple three-step process.

Step 1: Sharing

PLC participants must clearly decide which of the *Principles of Instruction* will be the focus of the meeting. This provides the timeline for execution of the strategy at least once before the reflection period. For example, if *clear goals* is a strategy that the school adopted as something that needs to be actuated in every classroom, every day, in every lesson, then the PLC would focus on how each teacher is meeting that target beyond simply putting an essential question on the board, which satisfies only an administrative check-off during a walk-through.

Clear goals that are tied directly to the curriculum and what students need to learn are not what most teachers struggle with; rather, it's their significance and relevance to student learning tasks. Since the advent and continual focus on standardized curriculum, clear goals and objective have been prominent; however, in the case of this PLC, how teachers use the goals throughout the class, tying them back to the task; how they routinely refer to them during the lesson; and how they ask higher-order thinking questions related to the goals are the primary focus of the conversation.

This collaborative experience is supported by each teacher's contribution to the learning community regarding how the teacher used the strategy within the classroom to support student learning. The closed-loop communication system begins with each PLC member sharing his or her experience with using the strategy, one at a time.

Step 2: Feedback

The second step requires each of the PLC participants to comment on what was said about the use of the strategy. They get to ask probing questions like "How did you know that the students understood the goals once you communicated to them?" Or, they can provide direct feedback like "Next time try to get more than one student to share their understanding of the goals." This leverages the power of a closed-loop system by discussing the intent of the strategy and how well it was effectively used within the class. This process uncovers and capitalizes on the collective knowledge of the group, and it's a three-part reflection model for each person as he or she shares—reflect to share, reflect to provide feedback, reflect on feedback.

Step 3: Reflection

The last step simply requires the teachers to reflect on the feedback that they received during the PLC and implement new ideas in the future. This practice closes the loop and brings the instructional cycle full circle. Teachers learn the strategy, implement the strategy, reflect on the use of the strategy, discuss it with peers, and then use the strategy again with new techniques and ideas.

Leadership Team Guiding Questions

1. How well did I execute the instructional focus, and what activities did I incorporate to do so?
2. What obstacles did I face during the lesson?
3. What adjustments would I make for next time (based on reflection and/or feedback)?

Chapter 6

A Reputation That Stands Out

If you possess natural leadership ability, people will want to follow you. They will want to be around you. They will listen to you. They will become excited when you communicate vision.

—Maxwell (1998, p. 79)

Leaders generally exude a series of qualities that make them easy to follow and attractive among the crowd. Their ability, respect for others, courage, success, loyalty, and value position them as people who stand out as exemplars of what it means to be successful (Maxwell, 1998). In schools, we want the right people to emerge, showing others the way forward. In doing so, they spread their reputation and that of the school culture as a place to do your best work, recognized by peers, leaders, and the community. In our first of two "standing out" sections, you'll meet a teacher who demonstrates, in action, what it means to be the archetype, which is how teachers and schools create magnetic reputations and winning teams.

STANDING OUT—WHAT THE ARCHETYPE LOOKS LIKE IN ACTION

Allow us to introduce you to Glenn Veit. Glenn is a real person, although his incredible attitude and positivity are almost too good to be true. We don't exaggerate his story; rather, if there's any exaggeration, it's actually a downplay of who Glenn really is and how he behaves and contributes at school, in service of his students and fellow teachers. It's incredibly difficult to characterize someone like Glenn with words, but for us Glenn is a perfect example

of what we mean when we say "archetype" and whom we want on the team
to build our "reputation."

Glenn Veit is an English teacher at Meredith Middle School. He's
everything that a school leader wants in a teacher from his interper-
sonal skills to his pedagogical prowess. When you ask Glenn, "How
are you?" in passing in the morning, his answer is never different:
"I'm always good," he'll say with a smile. It's not a hoax or some
feeble attempt at power talk; his response is genuine. When he introduces himself, he says, "My name is Glenn Veit, and I enthusiastically
teach seventh-grade English at Everett Meredith Middle School." He's
authentic and positive all of the time that it's actually startling, even
questionable, but it is real. Even if discussing a difficult situation, a
toxic colleague, or a disruptive student, he maintains the utmost professionalism, never reduced to gossip or negativity. He sees the good and
positive in everyone and every situation.

But positivity alone is not enough, and this is why Glenn truly stands
out. He masterfully combines his optimism with the powerful qualities
we associate with that of a teacher archetype. He is kind. His work ethic
is second to no one. He desires to improve every day. He invents new
ways to engage students in school and uses extracurricular activities.
All in all, he's a gem. At Meredith, he created an after-school program
called "Strategic Gaming Club," and kids stay after in droves to play
chess, checkers, board games, and more. His ability to connect students
to the school in meaningful ways is uncanny.

Glenn's talents don't stop at his ability to create incredible relationships.
In any given year, his students attain the highest student outcome results
in English Language Arts (ELA) as compared to any other teacher in any
other grade. His students make the most raw growth (points scored), they
make the most performance target gains (jumps in target brackets), and he
has the highest percentage of students meeting proficiency. When you ask
him how he does it, he says, "I always have such great kids; they work
so hard." His efforts lead to optimal performance. He is guided by clear
principles of instruction and a willingness to collaborate with colleagues.

Glenn's attitude, behavior, and skills manifest in success. He creates
his own archetype and provides the example for us to build based on what
he provides for the school community. The beauty in having a defined
archetype, and knowing the power of magnetism, is that as we aspire to
be more like Glenn, even if getting there is elusive with a near miss each
time, we'll be better off than we are today in working toward that end.

Glenn is our archetype, and with his qualities, talented teachers and community members find out about his school. Because of his character, he creates an allure and curiosity for wanting to join the Meredith team, regardless of whether a position is available.

Every school deserves and needs an army of Glenn Veits, teaching every student in every classroom. Moreover, students deserve for us to be working toward attracting, recruiting, and hiring more Glenns. It's precisely the reason for the excitement behind being guided by the archetype, defining the qualities needed to transform the performance of your school and to gain the reputation necessary to attract top talent. This initial step of knowing precisely whom you want and why positions you to build your winning team.

READY, AIM, HIRE

A recognizable brand and a powerful culture, including a complete archetype of your desired teaching staff, are the necessary initial prerequisites to hiring and influence. Having the conditions and reputation to attract talent is critical for what we do *before* we have a vacancy, but moving into the *during* hiring phase requires a host of tactical next steps. Although hiring is a procedural and even legally natured task, we have to maintain excitement and enthusiasm throughout the process, from the job posting to interviews to onboarding, always keeping in mind how electrifying it is to bring new people onto the team. Hiring holds the greatest chance for organizations to reach their goals and to impact student achievement.

An approach to hiring through extreme readiness takes time and out-of-the-box thinking. Education still has a long way to go. But we are beginning to scratch the surface with incentives and new ways to reach a broader audience. As our industry grows in this area, and our systems are set up to reward talent, we are more likely to recruit the right people for our open positions. As this happens at a faster rate, we must also advertise our innovative thinking as the new path forward. Progressive reform efforts in the area of human resources, which make the difference in both our hiring practices and the way in which we tackle student achievement, will make our efforts more rewarding and potentially curb the teacher shortage that impacts so many schools and districts.

"Compared to other popular education reform, such as reduced class sizes, incentives provide more than four times the amount of student improvement per dollar spent" (Ahn & Vigdor, 2011). When we incentivize the position with perks and peaks, advertise the role in new and different ways, and glamorize the hiring process for the candidate and the existing staff, we create the conditions that support the formulation of a winning team. Recruiting must be strategic, active, visionary, and ongoing. You *ready* yourself with your reputation, you *aim* with an open position, and you *hire* in an active and strategic way.

Chapter Focus Questions

1. Where do you see your archetype in action?
2. Which teachers in your school embody the true nature of your archetype?
3. How can you further promote your archetypal characteristics throughout the staff to excite others about the vision?

Chapter 7

Bringing Excitement to Human Resources

It is amazing that as we move further into the twenty-first century, most interviews are still the same stilted, rehearsed, and predictable conversations they were forty years ago.

—Lencioni (2016, p. 176)

Schools are microcosms of the community in which they reside, and as the town of Passel was reeling from a down economy, Pembroke High felt the effects as well. The school was in need of basic routine care, and classrooms needed basic resources. Despite the situation, Pembroke administrators stayed grounded, doing what they could to support the faculty and serve the students. One meaningful way in which they made a difference was by always being a voice for the school and the students, constantly talking about their great achievements, no matter how dire the situation was for the town or the school. Then during a town hall meeting, the principal first heard that a large biotech firm was opening a branch in the neighboring area. Pembroke High administrators knew this was a chance to be responsive to the community and to aggressively revitalize the curriculum by eliminating various electives and introducing a robust biotech pathway. School officials knew that the textiles and manufacturing industry no longer represented the economy, nor was it relevant to the business direction of the community. Still facing budget deficits and waning resources, the school sought meaningful and affordable ways to realize its new direction. Pembroke's principal believed that even though this would be an exciting proposition for students, and could be a great opportunity for them, the biotech programs alone would not be enough. He realized that the true difference would be in the person teaching the course and growing the program. For sustainability and a new direction, the school needs to recruit the right teacher.

The school sought to hire a dynamo to lead the biotech pathway and develop a robust curriculum, aligned with industry standards and tied to advanced placement courses and dual enrollment opportunities. Pembroke already had a good reputation, but as various schools were popping up in different areas, the administration feared complacency would lead to stagnation, and stagnation could lead to further reduction in enrollment. Low enrollment could mean closing its doors. The principal used unconventional methods to seek out the perfect candidate. He had no illusions about how hard it would be to recruit a rock star from a booming industry with great opportunities. Therefore, he took his time developing the perfect job posting. He sought out industry experts for their input and was transparent with them regarding what Pembroke was embarking on. His guerilla-style marketing and recruiting efforts led him to receptive and influential people within various STEM-related industries, many of whom promised to spread the word about the program and the need to fill the vacancy. The principal's passion was evident, and his enthusiasm regarding the possibilities inspired everyone with whom he spoke. At the end of the day, Pembroke wasn't looking to hire just a teacher for a new position; it was looking to revitalize a town, contribute to a rebounding economy, and alter the lives of children. Hiring the right person was essential to those efforts and required tactical steps to creating the right pool and patience in selecting the perfect fit and glamorizing the role and the possibilities of a bright future for the school.

The principal's efforts paid off, and the team was able to recruit the candidate they desired. To date, she's delivered in every possible way, expanding the department twofold, which now serves over 140 students in the pathway and several others who desire to take various electives that it now offers. Most important, the teacher believes in the program, in Pembroke as a great place to work and learn and its students as its number one asset. A somehow forgotten art of human resources was restored by the leaders of Pembroke who knew instinctively that great teachers don't just apply for open positions; they need to know that the school is ready to accept them and that they will be valued on their path to joining a winning team.

SPECIALIZE

The human resources (HR) department has critical functions in schools and districts, and yet, too often, it is not viewed or appreciated as a distinct and separate division within the organization. HR departments have a tendency to devolve into a reactive body addressing various employee problems and vacancies rather than proactively functioning within the critical domains of employee management.

There are four justifiable reasons for this: (1) Human resource departments are often too small and ill equipped. Due to the spikes in hiring that define human resource work in school districts, it's not the first place we look to staff sufficiently. (2) Human resource departments are typically staffed by former school personnel, many of whom were exceptional leaders, but we often find former principals and school secretaries in positions that demand an understanding of labor law, bargaining agreements, and benefit packages. If we're not careful, we can end up with an expertise deficit in a critical aspect of our organization. (3) Schools often rely on a central office to deal with employees, particularly the hiring and firing of personnel. Some state departments have even stepped into the recruitment and hiring function for schools. This overreliance on outside individuals and entities can leave schools in the lurch, reacting when they should be planning. (4) Finally, but certainly not the least, the major priorities of a human resource department in an educational system are often downplayed and not viewed as exciting or attractive in any way. That doesn't have to be the case; the essential functions of an HR department are the keys to building a winning team.

Browne (2017) admits that too many HR administrators feel the need to apologize for their role. The sentiment is that the job itself becomes a martyr of the organization, experiencing "untold levels of suffering to meet the common good of the people." We have to shift this unfortunate reality if we're going to thrive with quality people and pursue better, and more creative, ways to find the team members needed to accomplish our goals. This requires a newly found focus on HR in terms of both elevating the critical role of HR and creating a sense of "fun" and "joy" with the functions of the role, implementing stronger strategies for performing the key operations.

Undoubtedly, the breadth of the job is daunting, "tasked with being knowledgeable in employee relations, recruiting, compensation, benefits, employment law, federal and state regulations, training, organizational development, etc." (Browne, 2017), but that should not prevent us from lifting these essential objectives with creative and fun ways of thinking about the power and purpose behind them.

Fortunately, we can actually capitalize on what Rabe (2006) calls the "paradox of expertise." The incongruent nature of expecting someone to be experienced and skillful in all of the professional duties associated with HR essentially establishes the freedom to be innovative. Because "what we know limits what we can imagine," the absence of a full scope of knowledge provides space for new thinking (Rabe, 2006). And, to capitalize on this truth, and strengthen our innovation skills, we can look beyond our past practices and even our own profession.

As you try to do something special, exciting, important in your work, as you work hard to devise creative solutions to stubborn problems, don't just look to other organizations in your field (or to your past successes) for ideas and practices. Look to great organizations in all sorts of unrelated fields to see what works for them—and how you can apply their ideas to your problems. (Taylor, 2011)

Recruiting top talent for our winning team requires breaking the mold of most limiting HR practices in schools and districts. By adjusting and changing our thinking about HR, the primary functions of the role can be viewed as more glamorous, more exciting, and much more fun.

Small shifts in the way we think about recruiting people will lead to new ways of advertising our jobs for hire, incentivizing people to want to work for your school and district, and developing key supports for enhanced performance. The bottom line is that we must revolutionize our recruitment efforts in education to meet this exciting and challenging time for the future of our students and our schools.

Building a winning team is an ongoing and unrelenting process. It's the reason why we ground our hiring philosophy on the well-known reading structure, using the *before*, *during*, and *after* strategies for approaching and understanding any written piece. This translates perfectly into our revamped view of HR. *Before* our positions are open, we need a reputation that attracts people. That takes deliberate practices. *During* the hiring season, and when there are vacancies, we need excitement and inspiration. *After* the right people are in the right positions, when our team is established, we need structures for support and growth.

As a second tenet of this book—something that we learn from the former chief talent officer of Netflix—we posit that we should always be recruiting, always (McCord, 2018). This outlook and effort toward recruiting is not just about bringing people into the organization when there is an opening; it's active and ongoing, permeating the culture of the organization, even when vacancies aren't open. It's about the *right* people with a combination of specialized skills that uniquely complement the school. When we are consistently on the lookout for that special person with a special background and unique experience, we build a team, over time, that is unstoppable.

Too often, our search for talent limits us to thinking solely about skill and technical competence. Murphy (2012) asks readers to shift their approach to hiring, from looking for people with *proven ability* to a search for employees with the right *attitude*. In fact, he says that only 11 percent of new hire failures are the result of a lack of technical proficiency. The biggest issue is actually their inability to "implement feedback from bosses, colleagues, customers, and others" (Murphy, 2012). For these reasons, we must institute a *go slow* approach and be patient when we're recruiting staff to join our teams.

Go Slow

Hiring is a complex process, and it requires an incredible amount of time and attention when done well. It starts with the hiring team "being absurdly selective in who you hire" (McKeown, 2014), and it means going slow when our instincts tell us to move quickly. There are two alluring reasons why we are apt to hire faster than we should: (1) As hiring managers, the task is completed when we've onboarded the new employee. (2) The vacancy causes more work for the team due to the unfulfilled responsibilities created by the empty position. Both reasons are the result of a compulsion to act swiftly and fill the void, but neither one is actually helpful. But, by unpacking the reasons why we typically think this way, we can see our vacancies differently and slow down.

First, the role of the selection committee must be clear; thinking that this hiring team's role is simply to select and enlist the top candidate from the applicant pool is way too narrow of a scope for elite recruiting practices, which we address in this chapter and the next. In addition, the responsibilities of the hiring team need to shift. Hiring teams need to pivot their thinking from *hiring* as the task to *searching* as the responsibility.

This subtle yet important adjustment slows the process down because it recognizes that we may not select anyone at all. This is an unfavorable predicament but is far better than hiring the wrong person. To achieve this, we must, then, change our vocabulary from *select* to *seek* or *search*. Teams should not be formed to simply interview candidates, creating the notion that "today we will select from a pool of people who applied for the open position." Rather, the team's thought should be "Today we are in search of the right person to join our team"; it sends the message that if we don't find the right person, we don't have to select anyone, which slows things down.

Second, thinking that the vacancy is burdening the team is accurate, but the actual burden will be far worse if you hire fast and select the wrong individual. Even in the case of a vacant teaching position during the school year, it only gets worse if the wrong person comes on board. The solution is never to hire a mediocre teacher, who, you pray, does an okay job. We understand how difficult a vacant position is and how taxing it can be on every facet of the school. We know what you're thinking: What about safety? How do I cover the class? Who teaches the students? Who does the lesson plans? Who delivers the instruction? Who grades the papers? Who calls the parents? Yes, all of these important jobs need to be covered in the absence of a staff member, but in the case that you hire a dud, you'll end up with the same questions except the answers will be terrible plans, awful instruction, inaccurate or missing grades, and angry parents. The team's time is better spent filling the gaps than hiring too quickly for comfort.

"The bigger goal here is that you have set up a slow hiring practice that helps you avoid costly hiring errors" (Page, 2014). Frankly, if you don't spend your time going slow to hire the right person, the cost in time and the price you'll pay will be dedicated to the human resource side of performance appraisals, documenting issues, and working toward an exit strategy. The damages caused by a problem employee far exceed those of a vacancy, yet we convince ourselves that we need to fill a position, so we rush the work. Go slow, be patient, even to the extreme of keeping the vacancy open and filling it creatively from within until you have the right person onboard.

Keep the Vacancy Open

When you're recruiting top talent for your school, remember that a good substitute teacher is always better than a bad permanent hire. By no means are we implying that there should be a "tryout" period or trial time. That goes against our core belief of creating a reputation that attracts top talent for when you need to hire; when talent comes knocking, take every measure to bring them on board. But the reality in education is that hiring generally happens in the summer to prepare for the upcoming school year.

Teacher migration occurs between mid-May and August, leaving school officials with a short window of time to hire. This can be exhausting for hiring managers, especially when that same time is dedicated to planning and preparing for the upcoming school year. This flood of activities within a condensed time frame can result in making mistakes. Under pressure to fill a position, hiring managers might "hire quickly, thus poorly, because they need that warm body" (Trimarco, 2017).

Rushing to hire and thinking that someone is better than no one is off base and gives a fall sense of security, especially if you can creatively sustain the classroom and the students' education through internal measures until you find the right fit. Actively developing a strong pool of substitutes and a cooperative and understanding staff to help fill in the gaps are two quick remedies to support the go slow mind-set.

We know firsthand the feeling of fear that school leaders have when they lack confidence in the person they're putting in front of students. It's scary and it undermines the responsibility we have to our learners and the community. But worse yet is living with a hiring mistake because you believed so desperately that you had to fill a position to start the year with a "whole" staff. But fight this urge and simply don't do it. Communicate to the staff and the community at large why there is a vacancy and that finding the right person is more valuable than filling a position.

In the meantime, actively seek a good substitute. Use these three outlets to look hard for a stopgap before you create an even bigger headache:

(1) Scrutinize the substitute list. Ask your teachers who were the best, more reliable, substitutes from the previous year. There are almost always good people who can fill the role while you continue to recruit. (2) Call your retired teacher-friend. We all know great teachers who are retired and who might want to spend a few months, even a year, back in the role. The best teachers always miss the job. Get him or her on the substitute list. And treat these folks like gems, diamonds in the rough. (3) Think outside of the box. If necessary, dismantle the course section and redistribute the students.

Do whatever you can to preserve manageable class sizes, and by bringing your key people together, you can discover creative ways to change the schedule. It's better to "get by" using a creative plan B than it is to "get by" with a botched plan A bad hire. And, if the school community understands the power and long-term value of the go slow approach, combined with a challenging but fun process for hiring, everyone will rally around to make sure the culture and climate is preserved for excellence.

INCENTIVIZE

Developing enticing job descriptions, casting a wide recruiting net, and leveraging the power of the Internet are all best practices that schools need to employ to successfully hire quality candidates. The question remains, though, that given the state of affairs in education with numerous vacancies, less certified applicants, and schools vying for the same candidates, are these efforts ever going to be enough? The short answer is "no." And this reality is more severe in high minority, low-economic areas where student achievement can be a daily struggle.

In response to this growing concern, many school systems have adopted appealing hiring packages to recruit teachers. This creates a new dynamic within human resources by forcing school systems to consider what they can offer prospective staff members over their counterparts. The idea of incentivizing teacher contracts is nothing new; in 2000, *Education Week* ran a piece on the fierce competition among schools and how many are working to "attract talent, districts and states are hiking salaries, adding signing bonuses, and beefing up benefits packages. Many are speeding up the hiring process and offering on-the-spot contracts to new educators at recruiting fairs. Some are even forming partnerships with real estate brokers to offer discounts on housing to make jobs more attractive" (Blair, 2000). All of these efforts have only increased in intensity since this piece was written, and schools continue to explore, pursue, and find new methods to hire quality teachers.

Schools and districts are also not alone in attempting to solve these issues. Some state governments recognize the dire situation and are introducing incentive packages to candidates who are willing to work in their school systems. Of the various ways in which this is being done, as of 2018, over 16 states have adopted service scholarships or student loan forgiveness programs to attract candidates in high-need areas. Two shining examples are Indiana and Nebraska. Indiana offers what it calls a Next Generation Hoosier Educators Scholarship, which is a $30,000 service scholarship for a five-year commitment. Nebraska instituted up to $15,000 in loan forgiveness, which targets shortage areas, and offers teachers $3,000 per year, beginning after a candidate completes two years of full-time teaching. Repayment is accelerated for teachers in rural or high-poverty schools (Espinoza, Saunders, Kini, & Darling-Hammond, 2018).

These examples not only reveal powerful partnerships among state agencies, which is critical to solving any number of issues but also demonstrate the out-of-the-box thinking that is necessary in handling the teacher shortage that 90 percent of America's schools currently face (Espinoza et al., 2018). Offering prospective candidates assistance money is attractive to recent graduates, especially when we take into account that the student loan debt in America is now over $1.5 trillion (Knowledge@Wharton, 2018).

These programs have the potential to recruit teachers but must acknowledge that the last thing that schools need are temporary fixes and volatile band-aids. Monetary rewards can create brief appointments rather than long-range solutions. Schools cannot afford to prolong another inevitable vacancy by simply allowing teachers to leave their teaching assignment, the school, and possibly the profession when their service requirement is fulfilled.

To build lasting professional relationships that go beyond the required timelines of incentives, schools must create strong retention practices so that teachers stay even after they fulfill their committed obligation. Designing a strong infrastructure of sustainability is imperative, which we discuss in greater detail in chapter 5 when we dive into the topic of teacher motivation. Nonetheless, "money talks," and so it has strategic appeal for those who use it well.

While these coordinated incentives are valuable, the pressure remains on systems to attract and recruit candidates by revealing the benefits of working in their schools, distinguishing themselves from alternative institutions. School systems can use simple and tangible incentives to make job openings more appealing and a little more lucrative, but it's naive to think that money alone will solve the problem. That said, money is a starting point to the needed incentives for teaching positions. The private sector has long been the proving ground for the allurement that comes with better pay, bigger bonuses, and popular perks. It's time for the teaching profession to catch up before it's too late.

Money Makes the World Go 'Round

The incredible educators that we know and with whom we work did not enter this profession for the money. In fact, many of them have inspiring stories behind their reasons for joining the ranks and can quickly share a quip about a teacher, a coach, or an administrator who made a difference in their life. It's for these reasons that they chose to make the difference in the lives of others, not money. Despite the genuine influence that most educators crave based on their own past experiences, teacher pay is a constant topic of discussion.

Teacher salaries are not a mystery either; most salary schedules are posted online and available for public interest. Prospective teachers and citizens alike can easily uncover what teachers make in any given school system. Granted, we fully acknowledge that there are other benefits to being a teacher, but teacher pay remains an issue in many cities and states around the country, particularly when the salary is weighed against the various challenges that the school system faces. This was evident in the teacher and school personnel strikes of 2018 and 2019 that included West Virginia, Colorado, Oklahoma, Arizona, and the Los Angeles Unified School District.

Regardless of your personal political affiliation or the position you take about government jobs, no one wants a teacher walkout, a public protest, or a teacher strike, but these situations are happening, and they reveal the delicate and tenuous nature of the current conditions in education. While some systems are responding with innovation and new strategies to attract teachers, others continue to suffer with shortages and weakening resources. Systems with the right mind-set to battle the need for more teachers are working to retain them by offering bonuses, especially for working in hard-to-fill areas where the problems afflicting schools are exacerbated.

New York City reached an agreement called the Bronx Plan, which can award teachers up to $8,000 annually for working in schools that typically fail to attract talent (Shapiro, 2018). In Fairfield County, South Carolina, school leaders attempted to stave off teachers leaving the district by offering $5,000 if they returned for the next school year (Self, 2019). These incentives are designed to confront the dire situations that plague many schools. They offer a monetary bonus for working in challenging or expensive areas, and they're meant to recruit teachers into schools that generally have a difficult time building a sustainable team.

While bonuses and incentives are not new, they are a calculated way to recruit teachers and demonstrate that the community has an interest in hiring quality staff to support its young learners. Some schools, districts, and even states are going beyond pay, pushing boundaries even further, with even more innovative ways to successfully recruit teachers by offering enticing hiring packages.

Hitting Home

In addition to bonuses and service scholarships, districts are looking beyond common incentives, offering various housing packages to entice would-be teachers. Whether it comes in the form of a stipend for housing or the district's own housing complex, innovative school systems are using this perk as viable means to attract, recruit, and retain teachers. In these cases, housing is considered within the greater compensation package and is designed to attract teachers to communities that are working to resolve a teacher shortage.

Although there is only anecdotal evidence to support the effectiveness of these programs, districts like Santa Clara Unified School District and the Dare County school system in North Carolina both built affordable housing complexes for their teachers and view the programs favorably as an added incentive for teachers (Loewus, 2018). The Santa Clara Unified School District is located in the heart of Silicon Valley where the average rent is more than $3,500 a month, which can quickly consume a teacher's entire salary.

The harsh reality is that many teachers simply cannot afford to live where they work, which forces them to look for employment in other locations or leaves them with other issues, like an unreasonable commute (Goldstein, 2019). Long commutes are not just problematic because of time; they come with indirect transportation costs, again, forcing teachers to find better working scenarios. Granted, housing programs require cooperation from a variety of decision-makers at the local, state, and federal levels, but it is not limited to affluent areas based on expensive options.

> The city of Battle Creek (Michigan) received a $1.5 million grant last year from the W.K. Kellogg Foundation to provide support for entrepreneurs and to strengthen struggling neighborhoods. The grant included $750,000 for a housing incentive program for BCPS teachers and central office and building administrators who commit to the district for three years and want to live in eligible neighborhoods, most of them on the north end of town. (Hernandez, 2018)

The power in these incentives is that concerned stakeholders are willing to come together to support schools and attract the best teachers.

These programs and initiatives are not favored by all, and there is no doubt that housing programs alone will not solve the shortage problem, but these efforts represent the required commitment, innovative thinking, and extreme resolve necessary to build great schools and systems. While the idea of a housing program may seem foreign or far away, it takes one leader, from any position, to start the conversation. Schools and districts with reputation, recruitment, and retention in mind are outpacing the rest and advertising their inspiring differences.

Chapter Focus Questions

1. How can you create a supportive and understanding work environment that embraces the go slow philosophy?
2. What data do you review that gives you an insight into your vacancy trends and your hiring needs?
3. What can your organization do to incentivize prospective teachers to your school?

Chapter 8

Casting Your Net

You don't stand a tinker's chance of producing successful advertising unless you start by doing your homework.

—Ogilvy (1983)

ADVERTISE

At first glance, advertising for an open position seems like a relatively simple process. And although it doesn't have to be complicated, there are critical factors to consider to ensure that the overall recruiting efforts are effective. Arguably, advertising an open position is taken for granted in education. We easily can fall into traps because hiring is often seasonal, toward the end of a school year, due to retirements, relocations, and turnover. We can fool ourselves into thinking that we don't have to be creative with advertising positions because every year a new crop of potential candidates leave their teacher preparation programs ready to step right into our vacant positions.

Having a primary hiring season and a direct feeder system from colleges is beneficial, but with fewer teachers entering the profession, we need to cast wider advertising nets to create a greater pool of applicants. "In 1975, more than 22% of college students majored in education—a higher share than any other major. By 2015 though, fewer than one in 10 Americans pursuing higher education devoted their studies to education" (Passy, 2018). This growing trend is a wake-up call for the educational community. As previously mentioned, schools must tell their own story to attract candidates, but this new dilemma also demands that our departments of human resources review their methods, processes, and mind-sets regarding posting vacancies and active advertising to recruit talented staff.

The unique aspect of advertising a vacancy is that it serves as the first direct connection a candidate may have with your organization as a prospective employee (Society for Human Resources Management, 2016). Earlier, we described the power of branding and marketing as primary methods to attract potential employees, but advertising with a well-written job description is an explicit communication about potential employment. One aspect of this process is developing excellent job descriptions that not only clearly represent the position and the ideal candidate but also include features that speak to those outside the traditional educational circle.

Seeking and finding candidates without a formal education degree who may be searching for a career change is a powerful way to staff schools. Done well, you can attract potential, highly skilled candidates who fit your job description. Advertising positions is the primary way to let outsiders know that you're hiring, and when articulated with clear, strong, and captivating (not exaggerated) language, we communicate, and even sell, opportunities and possibilities to a greater audience (Tarpey, 2018). People desire to be a part of something unique, special, and rewarding.

In her book *Thrive*, Arianna Huffington writes that "too many of us leave our lives—and, in fact, our souls—behind when we go to work" (2014, p. 22). This startling reality, coupled with the HAYS US What People Want Survey (2017) of over 2,000 employees, revealed that 71 percent of workers would take a pay cut for a better environment and improved working conditions. Education, one of the noblest of professions, can inspire and motivate individuals who may have never thought it possible to become a teacher. With creative methods of alternative routes to certification and teacher residency programs, countless individuals have left their careers to make a difference in the classroom. Powerful job descriptions spark curiosity and potentially ignite a flame.

Continuing with this theme of possibility, human resources must accept the responsibility that advertisements convey more than a vacancy, but rather the transformational nature of education and teaching, so that a broader audience is reached. Once we accept the challenge, the next piece of the puzzle is to guarantee that our message is being heard. Finding prospective candidates who are graduating from higher education programs is a common and simple process. Getting them to commit to your school and district is why we focus on branding, but the approach we are recommending with advertising is designed to also attract atypical employees.

Granted, the core subjects—math, ELA, social studies, science, and world language—make up the majority of our open positions, but schools have an array of diverse and unique jobs that need to be filled, which can range from career and technical education to teachers on a special assignment who work exclusively with youth in jeopardy of failing. To cast this wider net, schools must proactively seek candidates with a "find and engage" recruiting method and not the typical "advertise and apply" method (Rodriguez, 2017). This approach shifts our mind-set toward recruiting as an ongoing process that is not bound by time of year or open slots to fill.

This manner of recruiting redefines how we advertise and how we maintain a connection with potential employees. Schools typically have a heavy hiring season that runs from spring into the summer. However, once we embrace the "find and engage" method, by abandoning the view that recruiting is a single-season event, we put ourselves in a proactive year-round position for advertising our school as a place to work. Similar to athletics, human resources can have an off-season, a preseason, and an in-season.

Each season has a specific focus with tasks that make the recruiting process fluid and successful. Coupled with effective data analysis, schools can anticipate future openings, identify areas of need, and develop lists of potential employees who might fulfill the vacancy, need, and desired archetype. Using this approach, the off-season is a time of reflection. The key off-season tasks are as follows:

- Review and reflect on the effectiveness of advertising and recruiting practices.
- Review and reflect on the methods and procedures used to screen candidates.
- Review and reflect on the interview process.
- Review and reflect on the selection committee's interview skill set.
- Review and reflect on the new employees to determine if those hired truly match the job description and if they are successfully fulfilling the job responsibilities.

This is the time that we learn and grow as a human resources department by using a critical eye of refinement to continually improve the recruiting and hiring process.

The preseason represents the preparation necessary to be successful for the in-season time frame. During this period, key aspects of the actual hiring process are ironed out in the following ways:

- Analyze data to predict vacancies.
- Review previous-year applicants to see if they are still in the market.
- Create applicant pools based on present and future needs.
- Create and refine well-informed and skilled selection committees.

All of these practices must take place to have a successful in-season, which is where everything comes together. Essentially, the finale is where all of our efforts come to fruition, and we actively hire candidates to fill needed positions. During this time, interviews are conducted and staff are hired:

- Potential candidates are directly contacted.
- Job fairs are attended or hosted (both in person and virtually).

- Selection committees conduct interviews with the layered approach that we discuss further in this chapter.
- Staff are hired and onboarding takes place.

This approach capitalizes on the effective use of human resources personnel by creating a formula for success rather than a response to vacant positions. Each season supports and develops the others to supply schools with incredible staff. The hinge point, on which much of this process depends, is in the use of technology. With the greater advancements we've seen with technology and the expansion of the Internet, our ability to recruit has systematically changed. It requires us to reflect on how well we have actually leveraged these new tools to our advantage with recruiting top talent.

Leverage Social Media

To embrace the "find and engage" method, human resources departments need to leverage the power of the Internet. As Sackett (2018) describes in the *Talent Fix*, it's never been easier for businesses to recruit and acquire talent due to the Internet and our ability to find and learn about potential candidates due to the numerous job boards and social media sites that are dedicated to doing so (p. 3). It's no different in the field of education than it is for any other organization.

Social media sites can be actively used to inform potential candidates of upcoming vacancies and timelines. We can advertise for open positions outside of our own websites. If our desire is to build a diverse and talented staff, our techniques for recruitment need to be diverse as well. The *Teachers as Consumers* report indicates that 71 percent of educators who were surveyed interacted with Facebook in the last 30 days (Long, 2018). Not only is Facebook a great platform for marketing, but it can also be used to attract and recruit the next crop of teachers for your school. Aside from social media, using online sites, such as LinkedIn, indeed, K12JobSpot, and other vetted education job boards, is key to taking human resources into the 21st century.

Potential teacher candidates are unlikely to search your district's website, and unless they are local, they might not even know you exist. To reach the audience you need, recruiting efforts have to be scaled to a new level of outreach. Unless you're leveraging Twitter, Facebook, and other specific career-focused Internet tools, your team will surely suffer from the shortage of teacher candidates. With the right reputation and the critical mind-set to reach a broader audience, even when many schools are experiencing scarcity, you can enjoy abundance. It simply takes a new outlook and bit of elbow grease. It also takes travel to fairs that may be far from home.

Fairs Far and Wide

Another traditional way to recruit is through job fairs. The challenge with job fairs is that they are valuable only if high-quality candidates attend and if you, as a potential employer, stand out among the places of interest for the job seekers. A passive approach to fairs, coupled with fewer people entering the profession, can quell a once tried-and-true process. We contend that there is still a place for using job fairs to recruit but only if you create an edge.

Consider the power in Amazon's job fair, which took place in Romeoville, Illinois, where it accepted 20,000 applications in a single event. At the fair, people "united in the conviction that Amazon represented untapped opportunity—that a foot in the door could lead to a career of better-compensated, more satisfying work" (Scheiber & Wingfield, 2017). We fully recognize the unique capabilities that Amazon possesses as a dominant powerhouse and the difference between our industry and Amazon's, but it is its belief in what it does and its philosophy toward recruiting that matter.

This is where Amazon excels and where we can learn from it. It assumes full responsibility for hiring a great staff, and it goes to great lengths to do so. It's the effort and attitude that we admire and must aspire to emulate. If you truly desire a robust applicant pool filled with potential, then invest in your own fairs that attract people from far and wide. This may seem impractical, but if you continue to rely on others to host fairs and create your applicant pool, you're limiting your hiring effectiveness.

If you recruit teachers the same way that others recruit their staff, then you will continue to get the same results that others are getting—average employees with an occasional "superstar" (Bock, 2015). Hence, there are two strategies that make all the difference in your effort to build your team: (1) Search and attend as many fairs as you can find and show up with flare. (2) Develop your own fair and advertise it as far and wide as you can reach.

A creative way to switch up the process, attract a different crowd, and make this effort more manageable is by developing virtual career fairs. We've cited the capability in the use of the Internet, and yet another revolutionary way to launch your human resources department into the new millennium is by using virtual fairs. It's a dynamic less-expensive way to reach out to large numbers of candidates and target specific needs and even underrepresented populations (Huang, 2018).

Once you create an online connection with prospective candidates, you can promote and advertise the special ways that your school is making a difference through student achievement and community impact. Recruiting becomes a promising way that we tell our story at the same time that we're searching for new players to join our winning team. And when our pool of candidates are ready to shine and demonstrate their best, we must make magic with a newly revived fun format for selection.

GLAMORIZE

Incentives and long-reaching advertisements will bring the right candidates to your doorstep, and when they arrive for the interview, a big job awaits. Two parts of a single problem land in your lap that need to be managed well. The first part of the problem is how we view hiring in general. We typically don't view or associate the hiring aspect of our jobs with fun and excitement. Generally, hiring and onboarding is mired with policies, paperwork, and loads of other bland yet important operating items. By acknowledging this, though, we can shift the hiring functions of our roles to be enjoyable and even spiced up to a point of glamor and delight. In fact, recruiting should be wonderfully exciting work.

The act of recruiting new team members is exhilarating when we keep our purpose at the forefront—building a winning team. The second part of the problem is that in our search for new team members our focus is often one dimensional. We tend not to think internally, which results in missed opportunities from which we can capitalize to make shifts and move key players around. Vacancies hold a world of potential on the existing team, and through key maneuvering, we can complement and strengthen the existing team. Recruiting goes beyond just the new person and spills into developing the potential on the current staff to form a more complete team.

Perry and Haluska (2016) remind us that the single most important way in which we improve both performance and company culture is when we add new people or replace the current people on our team. And it's not just the new hire who creates the potential for better outcomes or stronger culture. The process and act of hiring have hidden benefits for positively influencing the team. Granted, the work associated with a vacancy is a laundry list of "to-dos" that include several activities: posting the job, screening candidate materials, selecting the interview team, calling prospective candidates, and scheduling a time for interviews. Amid this mountain of work and our desire to fill a vacancy, we can lose sight of all of the opportunities for internal moves, conversations about values and purpose, necessary training for the team, and other advantageous possibilities.

The makeup and complexity of a school can easily change over time. Not only do schools change, but also the staff within those schools change as years go by. Often, vacancies create incredible opportunities that can be managed from within. Let's start with internal moves, for example. When a vacancy occurs, the first strategic thought should be about shifting existing people around in the organization for increased effectiveness. There well may be someone already on the team who is well suited for the opening, and there might even be someone who desperately wants the job.

This is common among teachers who earn advanced degrees in school counseling and social work. The key is to look within first to improve performance and to create a better culture. Maximizing the talent on your team and filling openings with skillful internal candidates demonstrate an acute awareness of the needs and intricacies of the team and, in turn, can increase both effort and engagement among existing staff. Having "the right people in the right seats" on the bus is paramount to success in any organization (Collins, 2001, p. 41). This is a key aspect of recruiting because it might mean recruiting for a position that is different from the one left vacant. This also creates the allure of glamor because people within the organization know they are appreciated, understood, and viewed as skillful assets. Every time the team is left with an opening, it creates internal opportunities.

A vacancy is also an opportunity to focus on values. Core values should be front and center every day, especially when key decisions are being made, which can be used masterfully when recruiting. This becomes twofold for performance and culture: (1) We use the core values as the basis for interview questions, screening tools, and any of our selection criteria. We should literally ask direct interview questions regarding values as in "One of our core values is *Inspire Trust*; please explain how you would do that with students, parents, coworkers, and the community." (2) Because the core values are used at the interview table, they require the interview team to be introspective about how they would respond to the prompts and what great responses to the questions are. We create a thoughtful and engaging environment regarding performance indicators and school culture for both the interviewee and the interviewers, thereby glamorizing the process as well as what we desire in our candidates and our current staff.

The act of filling a vacancy is altered and moves from being transactional to transformational. Each aspect, from active recruiting to the actual hiring format, becomes a professional learning experience for the team. As we outline in the next two sections, the hiring format, the hiring team, and all of the layers we add to the process not only act as our mechanism for selecting our new team player but also build a stronger understanding, relationship, and connectedness among the current team members. Essentially, we are able to take a common practice, like hiring, and make it exciting while at the same time building a stronger team during the process. Every time we hire, our team is strengthened, not only because of an additional recruit but also because of the format we use in selecting from a pool of candidates who were attracted to our school through reputation, incentives, and advertisement.

Fun Hiring Formats

Three exciting days and seven rounds designed to choose players amid antici-pation and excitement, the National Football League's draft has morphed into a marquee event of opportunity and potential glory (NFL, 2019). Granted, teachers and administrators are not earning seven-figure contracts and most cannot run a 4.4-second, 40-yard dash, but hiring teachers and essential per-sonnel should be celebrated and given the reverence it deserves.

Schools are a last standing societal bastion that are designed to further our next generation of learners for a better tomorrow. When we're recruiting for a new position, we should literally create fanfare around the process and the people involved (candidates for hire and selection team). The process should be exciting and fun; after all, we're adding new recruits to our winning team. Imagine that you're creating an experience similar to the NFL draft or even a Broadway theater production tryout.

Unfortunately, traditional recruitment efforts are often boring and even dreadful. In addition, they don't work well (Lencioni, 2016). Dagdeviren (2015) calls for a new model for recruiting employees due to the "honest" problems that we all know exist. He reveals that "recruitment is problematic" for both the candidate and the organization (Dagdeviren, 2015, p. 27). "After a round of unsatisfactory dialogues between the two parties, the candidate suffers feelings akin to being left in the dark, exploited, having her time wasted or in the worst case, being unfairly judged" (Dagdeviren, 2015, p. 27). The recruiters can be left with emotions ranging from "apathy to anger," says Dagdeviren (2015), author of *Creative Hiring*.

With the right mind-set and applied excitement about building your win-ning team, we can glamorize the hiring process and emphasize the enormous contribution each hire makes for our students and the greater community so that we overcome the humdrum of the past. The following suggestions have proven to be successful in our experiences and go beyond the classic and common models.

First, always add layers. The one- or two-step hiring processes aren't enough. Interviews designed with multiple layers that provide a clear picture of the candidates' skill set are necessary to select top talent. Group interviews, interviewing all of the candidates in the same room at the same time in a Socratic style of answering posed questions, are a great place to start. They allow you to see a larger number of candidates simultaneously, which can narrow the pool, providing insight into how candidates respond to various thoughts and ideas. Best of all, they create a buzz. If you're feeling really adventurous, you can also hold networking events after the interviews for the candidates to get to know one another and the interview panel.

Another creative method is the speed-dating-style interview, which allows for quicker snapshots as a first round with a one-on-one personal touch. These types of interviews can be likened to icebreakers—they break the surface as a getting-to-know-you strategy before the more traditional interviews are scheduled. From these creative but basic starting points, your team can discuss and call back candidates for the next round, based on interest and intrigue. Undoubtedly, the multistep process takes more time and more effort, but similar to the NFL draft, you are not looking for just any 6'8" 397-pound lineman. You're looking for the one who will most fit your needs, complement your team, and position your students for success.

This approach gives the selection team a thorough understanding of the candidates and also creates energy and enthusiasm around the entire process. Both the candidates and the interview panelists feel the significance of bringing a new team member on board. In chapter 9, we take a *deeper dive* into some steps you can take for setting up both group and speed-dating interviews. The most important point to remember when glamorizing your *interview process* is to emphasize the *process* over the *interview*.

More than an Interview

Again, two distinct sentiments emerge when the interview process is effective: (1) Designed well, the process is just as beneficial for the current team as it is to onboard a new team member. (2) A traditional interview lacks glamor and excitement, limiting the intended benefits for team development and the ability to even discern who the right person may be. For these two reasons, we want to address five critical areas for your multistep process:

1. Communication during the interviews must be clear.
2. Choosing the selection committee is critical.
3. Training the interviewers' ear for what we want them to hear is top priority.
4. Asking the right questions at the table is paramount.
5. Adding layers to test actual skills and aptitude is a must.

Each area rounds out a glamorous progression of hiring techniques.

Communicating clearly as a leader is absolutely imperative because it influences the team members and their communication with one another. This truth applies to any circumstance or situation and is particularly important when hiring. The first way that leaders communicate is by being present. We advocate for empowerment and delegation as key leadership competencies, but the principal should always have a seat at the interview table. Others can be "in charge" of every facet of the process, but the principal should always be present when the selection of a new team member is being made.

This process puts the principal in a position to develop his or her existing team by honing their interview and selection skills, and it also creates the space for the principal to create a hiring process that is fun, exciting, and engaging. This is the first step to setting the stage in creating a culture that is focused on possibilities. Next, choosing the selection team must be treated as careful business. Because the selection team will have a ton of weight in who ends up on the team, the right people need to be at the table.

Choose your team based on two criteria: (1) They should have one degree of separation. The people doing the selection should be directly impacted by who gets hired. In other words, they should have to work with the person, making the decision all that much more important. (2) They should be your superstars. They should be your most talented team members. They epitomize your archetype and understand the school and department needs firsthand. These individuals help set the tone in the room and keep the expectations high for the newly hired team member.

Once your team is ready to go, they need training. The fact is that "the majority of companies don't train managers how to hire well, or at all" (Robinson, 2017, p. 16). Teams need training in question development, procedures for rating and ranking candidates, and protocols for debriefing productively. We deliberately call the hiring committee a *selection team* or *selection committee* because its work goes well beyond asking questions and taking notes. This team must embrace the school vision, core values, and archetype so that they can drive the conversation toward a common understanding of who the best candidate will be.

This requires a couple of key practices. Bring the team in well before the first candidates arrives to discuss *who* and *what* you're looking for in a new team member. Have the team write down the strengths, qualities, and character traits that you desire so that their listening is more focused. Also, provide an interview organizer with space for the selection team to take notes per response, and consider a ranking system for each candidate to be awarded points per response for an overall score. One word of caution: be careful not to let the score alone dictate the selection but rather use it as a guide.

These protocols are to create a standardized practice of selection quality and inter-rater reliability to guide the meaningful selection of a new team member. Last, but not the least, always remember to convey, up front to the team, that the selection team is choosing their top candidate, and all of their input is highly influential and taken into careful consideration, but the final decision rests with the principal and the human resources department. The goal is to assess the candidate and review his or her skills from a 360° vantage point.

Finally, add a performance assessment to the interview process that denotes a level of skill or aptitude. This added layer goes beyond the candidates' ability to answer questions well and has them demonstrate one or more of the critical skills associated with the job. The biggest flaw in any hiring process is that most of the experience relies on a question-and-answer-style interaction, which doesn't get at the heart of what it means to be a teacher (or any other vocation for that matter).

Interview processes that include having the candidates teach a lesson, live in the classroom during a school day, are a great way to determine their skill level and aptitude. If this is not feasible, then have them teach the lesson to the committee or complete a minilesson or performance task. Candidates can come early to dissect an Individualized Education Program (IEP), critique a lesson plan, write a letter to parents introducing themselves, or do any number of important tasks that teachers have to do on a regular basis that will help with the identification and selection of your new recruit.

The goal is to assess candidates' ability to perform specific job responsibilities and not just answer questions. The interview should leave the selection committee confident that they fully understand how the candidate could effectively contribute to the team. For learning to be whole, we don't just ask students what they think about a piece of literature or a math problem; we have them write stories and solve equations to clearly demonstrate what they've learned. The process is no different for hiring new staff members, and the depth of your plan will give the team a clearer indication of the candidate's fit.

Chapter Focus Questions

1. How well do your current advertising practices create a deep and talented applicant pool?
2. Do your hiring practices provide you with the level of insight and detail needed to select your next superstar?
3. Is your selection team skilled at interviewing and dissecting candidate responses?

BUILDING A WINNING TEAM:
THE HUMAN RESOURCES MODEL

Figure 8.1.   The Human Resources Model
Source: **Courtesy of Joseph Jones.**

Chapter 9

Taking a Deeper Dive and Employing a Technical Tip

Hiring

> One of the most important steps you can take in building a visionary company is not an action, but a shift in perspective.
>
> —Collins and Porras (1994, p. 40)

The actual "hiring season" in education is quite short, and as we've noted, schools aren't always aware of their vacancies in a timely manner. Couple this with a pool of candidates who know that the window is short and we've created a rushed process that doesn't always lead to a great fit. Schools can adopt two creative practices to learn more about a greater number of candidates in a shorter period of time. This requires a new perspective on hiring by breaking away from the traditional question-and-answer-style process.

DEEPER DIVE 2: GROUP INTERVIEWS AND SPEED-DATING-STYLE INTERVIEWS

The following is a step-by-step process for setting up group and speed-dating-style interviews. This deeper dive delves into the layers of recruitment so that you can either adopt or adapt these steps to suit your needs. The important part is that you use these processes to narrow down your applicant pool in an engaging and interactive way beyond just the common and sometimes flawed paper screening process. These layers improve your recruitment and selection process for two reasons. One, you want to see and hear from as many candidates as you can, and, two, you gather as much information as possible about each of the candidates before making a decision. The old one-and-done interviews are a thing of the past because they inevitably leave out potential candidates simply due to time.

Directions for Conducting Group Interviews

1. Using your pool of applications, do a reverse selection process. Normally, you would select the ones in which you have interest in and eliminate those who don't stand out. In this case, reverse the thinking to only eliminate anyone who either is not qualified or has glaring issues. The goal is to bring in as many people as possible. The ideal number is 20–30 candidates.
2. Call the group in and explain that the first round is a group interview. It's important that they understand the process of this first round and how the group round works so that there are no surprises when they arrive.
3. Prepare questions that speak to the heart of your school vision, purpose, culture, and what you're looking to achieve. Prepare only one set of questions, based on the number of candidates who confirm attendance. In other words, you need only one question per candidate. You'll see why in the next steps.
4. Print each candidate's name on a piece of paper, copy it, and cut them up into pieces so that you have each candidate's name on small slip of paper, twice. Then divide the set of names into two "hats." We typically use bowls of some sort or paper cups. You'll have two sets of every candidate's name in two different containers.

Joseph Jones	Joseph Jones
Principal EL	Principal EL
T.J. Vari	T.J. Vari

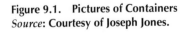

Figure 9.1. Pictures of Containers
Source: **Courtesy of Joseph Jones.**

5. Prepare the space so that your selection team is sitting at one table facing a long table for the candidates. In a normal interview, the panel would be facing one person; here, your team is facing up to 30 people (don't worry if it's only 12 or even 8; it will be worth the time you save interviewing all 8 people in the traditional fashion).

6. Create a PowerPoint or Google Slides with the following:

   a. An introduction slide
   b. A directions slide
   c. One slide for each question

7. Create directions. We use these: each candidate will have two questions to answer. We will pull your name twice to respond, once from each of our containers. We will call two names for every question we ask. When your name is called first, you get to answer the question first, which is a fresh question that no one else has answered yet. When your name is called second, you can respond to what the first person said with either confirmation, additional information that you would like to add, or even a disagreement with something that has been said. Each person will get his or her own question and the ability to respond to one other question.

8. Make name tents for each of the candidates so that the panel, and the rest of the people in the room, can identify who is speaking. This makes it easier for note-taking and eye contact. You can give the name tents to the candidates as they arrive, or you can have them set up on the table for clear seating arrangements.

9. Create a graphic organizer for the selection team. The organizer should have each candidate's name followed by two boxes for note-taking. The first box is for the candidate's first response, and the second box is for their follow-up response to another person's question.

10. Finally, on the day of the group interview, once everyone is seated, introduce the process, and begin with question 1 and your first selection. After the interviews are over, dismiss the candidates, thank them for their responses and time, and then deliberate with your team. You should be able to narrow the pool by half or even down to a final three people to call back for the second round, which may be more traditional or another layer depending on what additional information you need to glean from the candidates to make your best selection.

The process for group interviews is easy and fun. It helps you to create energy for the selection team as well as the candidates, and, most of all, it allows you to see a greater number of people in a shorter period of time to narrow down the pool to the people whom you need to spend more time getting to know.

Directions for Conducting Speed-Dating-Style Interviews

1. Much like group interviews, the first step is a reverse selection process. Normally, you would select the ones in which you have interest and eliminate those who don't stand out. In this case, reverse the thinking to only eliminate anyone who either is not qualified or has glaring issues. The goal is to bring in as many people as possible. The ideal number is 20–30 candidates.

2. Call the group to schedule the time and explain that the first round is a speed-dating interview. It's important that they understand that this first round is going to be quick, and they are going to be talking to a number of people individually. It's only fair to the candidates that they know what they are going to face during this scheduled time.

3. Gather your team to develop a list of questions. Use technical tip 2 to help with your questions. Prepare the number of questions for each member of the selection team to have a unique question to ask.

4. Develop a "notes page" for your selection team. Because they are going to have people rotating in front of them, it's critical that they take notes, including the candidates' names.

5. Prepare the space so that each selection team member has a table with a chair on each side of it, one for the selection team member and another for the candidate. All of the tables can be in one long row or numbered throughout the room as "stations" for each candidate to visit in succession.

6. Prepare a PowerPoint to kick off the speed "interview" date. Use one slide to introduce the selection team and another for the directions on how to "speed interview."

7. Assign a "leader" for the day. This person will use the opening PowerPoint and keep time for the rotation schedule.

8. On the day of the interviews, explain the process and then begin. Each member of your team will ask the same question over and over but to different candidates. The consistency in the questioning strategy allows for a deeper comparison than a typically scenario would allow. Rotate each candidate through the selection team stations/tables with three to four minutes for each question.

9. If you have more candidates than team members, create a holding space for when candidates are waiting to go to the next station. This can also be a space for them to network and talk to the lead interview who is orchestrating the day.

10. Finally, after dismissing your candidates, it's time to debrief. You can discuss candidates by question and per team member or by candidate names. In other words, either each selection team member shares his or

her findings about all of the candidates at once, or each selection team member shares his or her findings in a rotation per candidate.

These directions come courtesy of Dr. Keisha Brinkley, principal of Appoquinimink High School. Keisha runs speed-dating-style interviews in her library. Often with hundreds of applicants for one open position, she understands the importance of working to see and hear from as many of the candidates as possible. She uses the aforementioned directions for the first layer of her often three- or four-part interview process. She employs the "speed date" to get a sense of the candidates before committing to an even longer experience together; there is nothing more important than the people we hire to teach our students, so speeding through tons of people before spending more time with a smaller number of them is informative, fun, important, and applicable to the hiring process. Keisha shared that her team was once able to see twenty-four people in 90 minutes, which, using a 20-minute typical interview slot, would have taken close to 7 hours.

TECHNICAL TIP 2: HIRE FOR CHARACTER, NOT JUST CULTURE—THE BIG Cs

Throughout this book we've expressed the importance of culture and hiring people who will fit into your culture, expand the greatness of your school, and add to your winning reputation. Every person you hire plays an important role in "creating a less-than-average, average, or excellent school culture" (Casas, 2017, p. 16), which is why you need to add to your team only people who are committed to an excellent culture. But we advocate for one additional element within your hiring conventions, which is to hire for *character*, not just *culture*. "Character" is the other big C, and when combined with culture, the outcomes are endless.

The simplest way to demonstrate what we mean is by using Hirsch's (2018) "wrapper test." The wrapper test is simple yet effective in determining a person's character, and it's not the only indicator (nor should you base your decision solely on it), but it works:

> Before a candidate walks into the interviewing room, place a crumpled candy wrapper by the door. Then step back and watch: Does the candidate stop to pick up the wrapper or simply glide past it? You might still hire the person who walks by the wrapper. But you should definitely hire the person who drops it into the trash. (Hirsch, 2018)

Little tests of character provide tremendous insight into a person, and when you can test people when "no one is looking," you may uncover a hidden truth or two about them. No doubt this may be going a bit too far for some selection teams, but when the classroom door closes, you must be certain that the individual is the best person for your students. You can make that call about the wrapper test next time you conduct interviews. That said, your interview questions can be the right place to "test" a candidate's character, especially when you're not using a crumpled-up piece of paper by the door. We have two technical tips for the types of questions you should ask. First, address culture. Second, address character. Both of these big Cs are fundamental to selecting the right person.

First, the normal get-to-know-you questions like "Tell us a bit about your work history" or "Give us an example of a time when a student acted up in class and how you handled it" should not be used; in fact, they are best served inside the waste-paper basket with the wrapper. Neither question reveals a character or cultural fit, and usually the team doesn't learn much about the candidates from them anyway.

Most interviewees will have stock answers, including your typical edu-jargon, set to impress. But don't be fooled. The "prepared" candidate, in this case, might not be the best character fit. Instead, switch the format entirely, and don't ask questions at all. Use strong statements about your current and desired culture, and ask the candidate to respond. Make the statements aloud and say: "Tell us what you think about that." The following are two examples that can get at the heart of a *cultural fit* pretty quickly.

1. Each week our teachers get feedback from a supervisor in the form of specific praise, corrective action, and professional dialogue. Teachers are expected to engage by shifting strategies and discussing their lesson plans with their supervisor. Tell us what you think about receiving weekly feed-back and engaging in a cycle of inquiry about your planning.
2. We sent you our vision statement and core values ahead of today's inter-view for your review. Tell us what you think about our expectations for our school community.

Note that there are subtle tests embedded, like making sure that the candidate understands what some of the norms are in your school and demonstrating a degree of preparation prior to the interview. Both matter, and both speak to the panel as well, reinforcing expectations and cultural norms.

Second, the aforementioned cultural statements are critical, but we add a second type of response to get at the nature of a person's *character*, and this is where scenarios come into play. We're flipping the script here, as we often do, from asking candidates to respond with their own scenarios (as in the case of the aforementioned normal classroom management question) to providing the scenarios in advance. The following scenarios are examples of school-based vignettes to uncover a candidate's character.

1. Tell us about the most inspiring moment of your life. It does not have to be work related. We want to know who or what inspired you, why it mattered so much, and how it impacted you as a result.

2. Tell us about one person or group of people whom you aspire to emulate in your personal and professional life. Tell us about the person and why you aspire to be like him or her.

Character responses should be about *inspiration* and *aspiration*, two keys to unlocking the true nature of persons in terms of how they see themselves and how they wish for others to view them in life and work.

These questions address aptitude and attitude, not just skill and pedagogical prowess. We need teachers who can handle change, face adversity, and thrive with a growth mind-set, which is why we shift from a question-and-answer format to "Tell us about. . . ." This slight difference provides candidates with a platform to describe themselves in more detail versus the typical interrogation that interviews end up being, which often leads to short, canned, and prepared responses about work experience, higher education platitudes, and technical skills—all of which can be seen on paper during the screening process. You want prospective team members to tell you as much as possible about themselves, their character, and how they will help fortify an incredible school culture.

The good news, too, is that if you're paying close attention and you know what to look for, candidates often reveal their true nature in unique ways on their own. During one set of interviews that T.J. Vari and his team were conducting, the electrical power at the school went out. We reached out to the candidates about the situation and that interviews would still proceed as scheduled. One of the candidates called back to ask how many interviewers were on the panel. Then she stopped off to get a bottle of water for each of the team members, saying, when she arrived, that she realized that it could get quite hot (the interview was during the summer months).

Of course, the selection team could have glossed over such an incredible act of thoughtfulness and situational awareness, but it demonstrated the type of character we wanted within our culture, and it ended up being one of the topics discussed when weighing the options. She got the job.

LEADING WITH ENERGY AND ENTHUSIASM

Leadership requires energy and enthusiasm, and passionate leaders are driven to make improvements by bringing an identifiable energy to every situation and celebrating the team at every turn (Thomas-EL, Jones, & Vari, 2020). Hiring is a pivotal place where infusing energy must be intentional since the process can be mundane and consumed by policies and procedures that don't account for the construction of your winning team. Adjusting the typical recruitment process positions you to truly identify and select the right candidates for both a cultural fit and the character attributes that match your needs.

As a result, recruitment efforts are maximized by the three key accelerators: incentivize, advertise, and glamorize. Although each functions independently of the other, together they function harmoniously to bring more talent to the table so that you can build your winning team.

In schools, teaching positions are what Wintrip (2017) considers to be "core roles." This means that "an open seat creates an immediate and negative impact" (Wintrip, 2017, p. 133) until filled. Vacancies can create panic, which is the opposite of what you want in a measured thoughtful program of work, which is necessary for hiring. This is why we organize the hiring process into three distinct parts—*before* hiring, *during* hiring, and *after* hiring. The parts allow you to see each aspect with clarity so that you can approach it with precision.

The recruitment—*during* hiring—is more complex than just interviewing and selecting the best person, but executed correctly, it also doesn't have to be complicated. If the right strategies and techniques are effectively employed, hiring can be engaging, fun, and fruitful in your efforts to build your team. It means that we must eliminate the passive and traditional approach of the past. The one-dimensional process, singularly focused on filling a position, lacks energy. Instead, leaders are obligated to adopt an active recruitment strategy that will enthuse the team, develop them beyond the classroom, and bring on the best people for your vacancy. Getting the work done—recruiting top talent—takes measures of precision. It means knowing what you want in the position and being strategic in your selection process.

Smart and Street (2008), authors of *New York Times* best seller, *Who*, tell readers that "the first failure point of hiring is not being crystal clear about what you really want the person to accomplish" (p. 20). Hiring should be exciting and fun because you are not just filling a vacancy; you're hiring for possibility. Hiring the right person puts you in the best position to meet your goals and fill the voids and gaps that currently exist on the team. New hires bring a wealth of potential that can range from pedagogical expertise to innovative ideas. Systematically approaching the hiring of candidates bridges where you are now to where you want to be in the future. That said, precision is the name of the game, and it takes a team of your current leaders to build the team of your future leaders.

Chapter Focus Questions

1. What opportunities exist for you to revamp your interviewing techniques?
2. How well do you build a level of energy and enthusiasm around the hiring process?
3. During the interview process, how clear is your team regarding the "fit" of the candidate?

Chapter 10

Recruiting Elite Talent

Another way to prepare for your shining moments is to study those who have gone before you, and ask questions of people who have more experience than you.

—Carroll (2004, p. 74)

PRACTITIONER SPOTLIGHT

Lynn Colón told us an extraordinary story about her time as principal and all that she did to recruit top talent to build her team of teachers. Colón, now the director of the Office of English Learners Programs and Services, had a vision as the principal of Mary Williams Elementary located in Dumfries, VA that the school's culture would emulate Disney World. She knew that if she desired to attract staff members who would share her Disney vision, she needed to use Disney-style hiring practices.

Colón told us that it all started with the vision, a vision to be fully ingrained within the culture. In her 2017 article in "EdSurge," she wrote that "staff are hired for attitude, not aptitude." She implemented business words and phrases like "guest" and "customer service" to refer to how all people should be treated in school. One thing that she did to really make the interview process special was to meet the candidates out for lunch. Her goal was to learn as much as she could about the prospective staff member by asking poignant questions to judge how well they might fit into the vision. She wanted to know about their passion, and she shared her passion as well. The idea was to "talk about what makes us both tick," she told us. She built her winning team by going well beyond the normal practices that schools use, and she "branded everything to fit the vision" that she had for a Disney experience. You can learn more from Lynn Colón by following her on Twitter @TheColon_s.

THE ARCHETYPE OF THE POSITION

In chapter 4, we discussed the creation of an "archetype" so that you have a set of attributes that you can use as a starting point for the reputation that you want your teachers to have and so that you attract a particular employee skill set when vacancies arise. The archetype activity is the first step in defining the personality traits, characteristics, and actions of a teacher.

Done well, it serves as a beacon, a guide, to asking yourself and your team to commit to the qualities that we all aspire to emulate at work. The archetype creation happens *before* a vacancy so that you can take the next critical step in truly defining what you need *during* the time when actual vacancies arise. Once you have the archetype of a teacher, a vital next step is to analyze any specifics of your openings to meet the particulars of the school's needs and to maximize recruitment efforts.

Having a teacher archetype is powerful, but schools would be remiss if they skipped the step that we call *position analysis*. This process couples the archetype with needs of the school and the opening, beyond just the general vacant position. Not doing so limits effective hiring practices in two ways: (1) You end up looking for a perfect candidate to meet all of your archetypal qualifiers. (2) Continuing to fill surface-level needs leaves many of the specific gaps unattended. In other words, your teacher archetype is the makeup of an ideal master teacher who brings qualities and virtues to the team, but it doesn't account for the details and nuances that comprise the position that became available or the skill gaps on the team due to the opening. Simply filling vacancies without addressing the acute needs of the school and the students will prevent you from creating the dynamic workforce that exists within every winning team.

Let's first tackle the problem in only using the teacher archetype to search for the perfect candidate without a detailed analysis of the position. Simply put, perfection doesn't exist. We are all searching for a "purple squirrel," the name that many human resource professionals dub for a completely ideal candidate. The problem is that these rare individuals are "almost mystical in nature" (Haun, 2013). The perfect candidate rarely exists and almost never materializes during the recruiting process.

Although we advocate for going slow and avoiding the "warm body" syndrome that plagues some schools, it's equally ineffective to take this to an extreme in searching for perfection. We have to accept that purple squirrels and unicorns don't exist. The good news about the archetypal characteristics is that they are attribute based, such as "integrity." For this reason, we hire through two distinct lenses: *the archetype of a teacher* and *the archetype of the position.*

The next problem we encounter when using only your general teacher archetype to define a vacancy is that it neglects the particular demands of the position. Vacancies always come with intricate details about the needs of the position, students, team of teachers, school, and even community at large. The more specific you can get in enumerating the needs you have in filling your open positions, the better equipped the selection team will be in making the best choice. Normally, we have a sense of what we need to take the team to the next level, but clarity on the specific areas must be explicit among all team members.

> You may have some vague notion of what you want. Others on your team are likely to have their own equally vague notions of what you want and need. But chances are high that your vague notions do not match theirs. (Smart & Street, 2008)

This is why the entire team needs to be on the same page about whom we want and how he or she will contribute to the success of the school. One creative way to do this is to make a list of the not-so-obvious needs that we have as a teaching team and an entire school community.

The truth is that you're not likely to fill every need identified, but you'll satisfy some of them and you'll know what pieces are missing. And, by knowing the specific gaps, you're better equipped to skillfully scour through the résumés for the right applicants to interview. It's critical that the entire selection team has a grasp of the positional needs that you're trying to fulfill. After all, they're adding a team member, someone with whom they will likely be working closely for years. This level of responsibility adds a layer of accountability for the team throughout the hiring process because it makes the selection far more personal and even that much more important.

The byproduct of this important process is trust. As you conduct your positional needs analysis with the team, you are also building and developing a bond, a level of trust, among each member. Trust is a fundamental aspect of teamwork, and vacant positions allow leaders to demonstrate and communicate how much they value the ideas and feelings that each team member has about the qualities and skills a person must possess to successfully fill the vacancy.

> You are not the only person who is going to have to work with this candidate. There is likely a team of employees you trust that will have to interact with him or her every day. Their opinion should matter. (Bryant, 2018)

This open dialogue and collaboration also leverages the diversity previously described, which takes into consideration any ideas beyond the norm. There are always basic functions that the position requires, but there are also many layers to what each person in a school does, which contributes to a positive culture and ultimately a successful school. In fact, it's often the ancillary roles we play that impact the culture of our schools more so than our primary assignment. Creating the archetype of the position requires us to go beyond the obvious needs that any vacancy creates. It produces a vulnerability about our current team and the true desire to be a better one in the future as we build.

Beyond the Obvious Needs

When a position becomes available in our schools, the obvious work is often the easiest to define for the advertising strategies that we discussed in chapter 8. But the team's analysis of the role needs to dig deep and go well beyond the obvious to recruit and hire the right person who can help take the school to the next level. There are a number of factors to consider. Let's start with experience. If your math department is entirely made up of inexperienced teachers, that fact should be taken into account as you develop the archetype of the position. The team may want to consider hiring someone who adds experience, pedagogical skill, and leadership to the group. This may or may not be a central focus or deciding factor, but it should begin to outline whom you're looking to hire more than just a "math teacher."

There are a number of other characteristics and qualities to consider, and we won't cover all of them in this book; that's for you to do with your team, but we do believe that there are few essentials. The first is leadership experience. In *Talent Magnet: How to Attract and Keep the Best People*, Miller (2018) reveals that finding people to fill positions is not nearly as concerning as their actual caliber. In schools, we don't just need subject matter experts; we need teacher leaders, motivators, and connectors who can move the work forward in ways that principals and assistant principals simply don't have the capacity to do without a strong team (Fullan, 2014).

For this reason alone, the experiences of the candidates you are recruiting should be a top consideration. When recruiting teachers, we need to look for versatility, adaptability, and responsibility. They should have demonstrated experience in leading in their former role, and in the case of new teachers, they should have leadership experiences from high school, college, civic responsibilities, and elsewhere that is evident on their résumé.

Next, there are always departmental needs and the grade-level composition to examine. More than anything, you want to assess the diversity in any group where an opening occurs. As we discussed in chapter 4, there are extensive benefits to a diverse team, and this means analyzing the gender, race, ethnicity, experience, and age diversity within each department and grade level. The goal is to ensure that the department can connect with the students and one another for maximum impact. Consider the use of professional learning communities (PLCs), which is a norm in most school systems. These communities thrive and achieve optimal performance through diversification.

The powerful aspect of diversity is that it can go beyond the typical identifiers. In your quest, you should also try to uncover a candidate's cultural intelligence. Having cultural intelligence means that you can interpret the otherwise unfamiliar and ambiguous actions of others in the same way that their peers might (Earley & Mosakowski, 2004). Because this is a quality that can be learned, you can search for experiences within a résumé or interview that allow you to assess the candidate's level of cultural aptitude. In this case, you're specifically looking for experiences that demonstrate the job seeker's ability to work in environments that are clearly divergent from their own.

Finally, hiring must move beyond the immediate team and consider the entire school community. Influential new hires make an impact well beyond the classroom. They serve as coaches, club advisors, committee members, and more. The school may be experiencing the need for an after-school program for young girls. Programs, like *Girls on the Run*, whose mission is to "inspire girls to be joyful, healthy and confident using a fun, experience-based curriculum which creatively integrates running" may be filled by a new hire. The actual job posted is just the minimum qualification when recruiting top talent. The only way to have a real team of winners is to assemble a group of people who each play a unique role by contributing to the school community in a variety of ways for the achievement of the greater mission of the school.

A Team of Winners

When you use the archetypal approach for both *the teacher* and *the position*, you create a team of A-players who fulfill the individual roles needed to bridge the gaps and shortcomings among staff to positively impact student achievement. This strategic approach also counteracts a typical and limiting belief that not everyone on our team can contribute at high levels. We need to eliminate our bell curve mind-set regarding employee talent and service.

Team construction is never really about a group of all-star players but rather each individual's fit and contribution to the team. In *A Band of Misfits*, Baggarly (2011) tells the story of the 2010 San Francisco Giants as the most unlikely team to win the World Series. Nicknamed the Dirty Dozen, the players came together to prove something about greatness, which is that talent alone is not enough. Rather, it's about teamwork and how each person uniquely fits together to compose a masterpiece, bringing success into reality. The whole is always greater than the sum of its parts.

And there are thousands of examples where a winning team is far more about perfect harmony than it is about an assemblage of all superstar players. Even the Chicago Bulls of the 1990s can be considered in this light. Sure, they had Michael Jordan, arguably the best basketball player of all time, but one person doesn't win championship after championship on his own. The Bulls were a threat because they were a complete package, coached by legendary Phil Jackson. Each aspect of the team, both offensively and defensively, was complete, and their desire to win was more important than any one person's contribution.

Our favorite example is the 2018 Philadelphia Eagles. Their Superbowl win demonstrates how teamwork, fit, and desire can outshine the competition every time. Jason Kelce's powerful underdog Eagle's parade speech walked listeners through every reason why the Eagles should not have won that year. The irony is that these reasons were the ultimate combination in a winning team. This is precisely what you need as you recruit your next players—a consideration about the package, not the person. It's why generic and obscure job descriptions and hiring practices must be the thing of the past.

"Specificity," outlining clear expectations, is the new name of the game. The greater the clarity we have regarding what we need to be successful, the more likely it will be that we improve at a faster rate. Leaders must think of themselves not just as coaches who provide feedback for current players but as coaches who scout new teammates using the current conditions and needs of the team. This also means that we need to leverage the practices of other professions, including sports, as we work with our teams to uncover their strengths and weaknesses for appraisal and development.

LEADERSHIP TEAM ACTIVITY 3: TEAM STUDY

The best coaches, as Seth Davis writes in *Getting to Us: How Great Coaches Make Great Teams* (2018), regardless of their coaching differences, are persistent, empathetic, authentic, and knowledgeable. These four qualities are the backbone that drives the development of each remarkable team. For school leaders to be successful, they need to think like great coaches who build winning teams.

Regarding knowledge, coaches have two primary ways that they build their knowledge base to support their team: (1) They study their own team in terms of performance, culture, and agility so that they know what the team needs to do next to get better together. (2) They study other teams, especially the competition, to uncover the habits and patterns that make them great so that they can use that intel to their advantage.

The best coaches analyze the team's strengths and weaknesses with everyone at the table. They watch tape, study plays, determine strategy, and seek clarity together with the players to make practice more effective and to prepare for the next big game. School leaders can replicate both methods to create conditions for success on their leadership teams. We call this "team study." When school leaders use *team study* with the leadership team, it also helps with capacity building by developing their leadership skills and strengthening their roles as leaders and as teachers. It also helps everyone to uncover the "blind spots," which signals the gaps that the team can fill during the next round of interviews.

The better we know how our team operates, and how other successful teams operate, the faster we can move in the direction we want to go. As for the leadership team, they also need to think and act like coaches for their teams—students, departments, grade levels, and PLCs. This type of coaching synchronicity leads to "continuous improvement." Models and cycles of continuous improvement are always distributive, leveraging the skills of the entire team and creating a pervasive culture of excellence rather than pockets of success.

A productive team study is achieved by using two primary methods that can be done strategically during leadership team meetings. First, we must learn how to study our team's strengths and weakness, and, second, we must learn how to study other teams from other professions (including sports) to get better in our own arena. The bottom line is that to lead the future, school leaders will need the skills to create leaders (Kotter, 2012). Let's look at a few examples that you can use with your team. Each comes with one question to ask as a starting point for the discussion.

Watching tape—Every great coach watches his or her team's recorded video to play back how the team performed for review and reflection. In education we don't often think of watching tape with our teams, but it's a great strategy to build team efficacy and to identify specific skill gaps. You can watch tape with your team in two ways: (1) Search for short video clip recordings of teachers teaching a lesson. Some quality online resource are available from sites like Engageny.org that maintain a video library. As an activity at your leadership team meeting, show the clip and have everyone take notes regarding what the teacher is doing, what the students are doing, and the task itself.

The goal is to reserve judgment on the teacher's performance until the team agrees on what they observed. Then, each member uses your official teacher evaluation or walk-through tool to assess the lesson in a predetermined area, such as questioning techniques or student collaboration. In this exercise, you're using team study to uncover how everyone thinks about teacher performance and lesson execution. Not only is this a quality benchmarking activity to develop your team's reliability, but it creates an entry point for a discussion of what would make the school stronger.

Ask one question: What gaps do we have in our pedagogy that could be improved?

Data dig—Sports analysts look at data from every angle. They study the team during practice and in action. In schools, we often get fixated on lagging data points that tell a story about what happen*ed* versus what's happen*ing*. Studying your team during interim and marking period reporting provides critical insight into the current status of student learning and engagement, which allows for strategic adjustments and changes long before high-stakes test scores are available. At a clear breaking point, such as after marking period one, do a data mining activity by looking at vital data. We suggest the following list, but you may add other items to it:

- Discipline infraction numbers by incident, offender, grade level, location, demographic, action taken, and reporting teacher.
- Attendance summaries by student, teacher, grade level, and demographics.
- Teacher-reported grades by demographic, teacher, course, and percentage of letter grade earned. (Note: look closely at the percentage of Ds and Fs by course.)

Ask one question: What gaps in student outcomes data do we have at our school?

Parallel skills—Taking time to analyze and discuss another team, from sports or business, to draw parallel situations and learn new ways to approach culture can be both fun and useful. The key is to choose a sports team or business that either has a well-known culture or publishes insightful information about itself. Your team can discuss what it must look like, sound like, and feel like to work in that team environment and the qualities they can adopt. Some of our favorites are Pixar, Patagonia, Disney, Wawa, Google, Apple, FC Barcelona, New Zealand All Blacks, and Lady Vols. The good news is that the list is endless, and you get to discuss not only the team dynamics but the coach, CEO, or leader as well.

Ask one question: What gaps in culture do we have at our school?

Leadership Team Guiding Questions

1. What gaps do we have on our team that we can fill using our recruiting process?

2. Which sport teams and business examples do I want my team to learn from and emulate?
3. Who are the greatest coaches of all time, and what can we learn from them to be better leaders?

Chapter 11

Strategically Pursuing a Clear Path Forward

Leadership is the process of getting everyone to the place they are supposed to go.

—Blanchard and Muchnick (2003, p. 103)

PRACTITIONER SPOTLIGHT

Cleave "Bivins" Miller III is the principal of McAllister Elementary School in Richmond Hill, Georgia. We connected with him to learn more about the tips and tricks that he uses to recruit top talent for his awesome team. When we connected, Miller was responding to a surge of 100 additional students to his school, so his hiring practices needed to be impeccable or he was going to be in a desperate situation. From his experience, Miller accentuated three simple facts about recruiting: (1) plan early, really early, (2) screen applicants incredibly well, and (3) support the people we hire. He approached these truths with innovation and urgency.

Principal Miller plans his hiring tactics at the start of each school year. While many school leaders are kicking off the year with their new staff members in mind, Miller doesn't have that luxury and is moving past that phase, preparing to hire the next crop. Because of the growth at McAllister Elementary, planning is critical. He said that recruiting teachers can't be last minute or when a vacancy arises. Miller and his team search for college career fairs to attend, and they actively promote the school on social media. They use the "find and engage" method, always reviewing applications long before openings occur so that the right candidates are at their fingertips. And, once they make an offer for the person to work at McAllister, they maintain a relationship with the new hire until they come on board the following year.

Miller even provides a "swag bag" for every new teacher to immediately connect them to the school and make them feel a part of the team from day one.

Miller's interview and screening process is far from "normal" and is
designed to fully get to know the candidates. He uses Flipgrid online video
recordings where candidates are prompted to discuss their teaching styles and
professional goals. He talked about preinterview tools to expedite the process
so that valuable time is spent face-to-face with prospective new hires rather
than the entire pool of candidates. He even does pre-reference checks to know
more about candidates to prepare for the interview versus finding out more
about them afterward. In two words, he told us that recruitment is all about
"focus" and "timing."

Finally, Miller isn't simply intent on finding the right people to fit *his*
needs; he works to keep teachers engaged and happy so that they can be
productive for *themselves* and their *students*. Supporting their professional
goals, celebrating their individual accomplishments, and making sure they're
mentally, emotionally, and physically fit for the job are critical areas that he
uses to retain his teachers. This includes community partnerships with places
like the Young Men's Christian Association (YMCA) so that his team can do
group exercise activities together. More than ever, teachers are looking for
camaraderie and joy as two important workplace outcomes, and Bivins Miller
doesn't leave that to chance. You can learn more from Bivins by following
him on Twitter @BivinsMiller. Check out his article in the March/April 2019
NAESP publication, *Principal*, for even more great advice.

STRATEGY FIRST

Chess is said to be a game of pure skill forged in strategy. Josh Waitzkin
(2007), eight-time National Youth Chess Champion, recounts a particularly
grueling Nationals match where his game opponent started with an offensive
"variation" that he had never seen before, which quickly "devoured" him.
The "central pawn phalanx" left Josh reeling and searching for answers and
opportunity.

The aggressively assured style of his opponent caught Josh off guard and
off his game plan; he found himself playing from behind, not the best place
to be in chess. Incredibly well trained and with countless hours of preparation, Josh recovered. His skill and strategy emerged, guiding him by opening
his eyes to the board and opportunities that were several moves ahead. As
the match continued, he found an unlikely answer by sacrificing his knight
as well as his remaining pawns. Although "counterintuitive," it was the only
way to win, and in a final head-to-head king battle, Josh was victorious.

Pursuing greatness is no easy feat, whether it is in a chess match, teaching a masterful lesson, or building a winning team. Competition is fierce, and circumstances and conditions are always changing. Josh reminds us that in pursuit of excellence, regardless of the endeavor, a "well-thought-out approach that inspires resilience, the ability to make connection between diverse pursuits, and day-to-day enjoyment of the process" is what yields success (p. 29).

Similar to chess, an astute and judicious approach to recruiting requires extensive strategy. It's not about the immediate move ahead, the one you actually see, but rather the one around the corner and out of sight. Seeing the "board" several moves in advance clearly generates momentum and leads to success, but it also requires a well-developed and practical plan that begins with a keen understanding of the school's needs and the archetype of the position that is going to be filled.

The formula we described for recruiting—the advertise, incentivize, and glamorize model—requires an active approach to recruiting, with each fundamental aspect fitting nicely under the pivotal umbrella of strategy. For optimal recruitment efforts, we must be strategic with a skillful survey of the institution's needs, which include the key takeaways gleaned from a strategic process that discerns the particular skill sets that the candidates possess to meet the demands of the vacancy.

Each prospective candidate should possess the necessary qualities to fill the gaps and voids of the position for which they apply. Undoubtedly, we hire for vacancies, such as math and science, but, as previously established, this is a shortsighted view; only the skills, qualities, and characteristics of the person will amplify the school culture, aid in the teaching of the content, and masterfully help build relationships in the classroom. The ability to discern whom to hire onto your winning team requires a thoughtful and strategic process that fits into our seasonal approach to recruiting. Strategic planning falls into the preseason because it's used to seek clarity and understanding as we gear up for the games to begin.

There are a variety of strategic methodologies to evaluate organizations and analyze situations to yield critical information for useful decision-making. Although data is becoming more commonplace to inform decisions and to guide the development of strategic plans, many administrators could further benefit by using business analyses strategies to help them gain clarity and insight into various situations. Collins (2001) eloquently describes that businesses that are able to "conduct autopsies without blame . . . go a long way toward creating a climate where the truth is heard . . . [and] with the right people . . . you should need to only search for understanding and learning" (p. 78).

This truth-seeking approach can be utilized in schools by guiding the process with a proven, and simplistic, system like SWOT. The power lies in having a tool to organize and capture all the critical information to serve as a guide, to keep everyone aligned to the core values and purpose, which is especially important in an ever-changing environment (Harnish, 2014). Done correctly, tools like SWOT can focus efforts toward identifying critical information that can help guide leaders through thoughtful decision-making regarding any eminent need, which, in this case, is recruitment of key staff.

Strategic planning, coupled with a strong leadership team that leans on their collective understanding of the school, the students, and the community, can unearth hidden findings that might otherwise remain elusive to common problem-solving approaches. To dive deeper into what will truly advance student learning and the people needed to do so, the team must have an open mind, free from bias and premature judgment. SWOT provides a structured approach to analyze and "examine their company's internal *strengths* and *weaknesses* as well as external *opportunities* and *threats*" (Schoemaker, 2015).

Essentially, a leader can focus on a given area of the organization, such as personnel, and evaluate the various dimensions associated with the topic. In this instance, it could evaluate a recent group of hires or even the practices associated with hiring. The *S* and the *W* refer to the institution's internal *strengths* and *weaknesses*, while the *O* and the *T* refer to the external *opportunities* and *threats*. This bilateral dynamic requires the leader to look inward *and* outward to determine any necessary next steps in a strategic manner. Consider only the *threats* assessment piece as it relates to hiring and all of the recruiting efforts geared to creating a greater applicant pool.

By shedding light on all of the external threats, such as fewer college students entering teacher preparation programs, schools are forced to consider unique and different alternatives to solving the problem. This includes any of the huge glaring issues but also all of the small potential threats we assume as germane to any initiative. As Thaler and Koval (2009) articulate in *The Power of Small*, unique opportunities will unveil themselves as we pay close attention to the small but most critical nuances associated with our industry. Paying attention to even the smallest details and taking advantage of the smallest of opportunities can lead to great results.

SWOT is a simple formula, designed to extract thoughts and organize them in a systematic way, which is commonly presented in a quadrant-style depiction in figure 11.1.

1. *Strengths*—The internal factors that make an organization or initiative more competitive than others with similar attributes.
2. *Weaknesses*—The internal limitations and issues ingrained within an organization, such as any factor relative to losing ground against another organization or way of thinking regarding a problem.

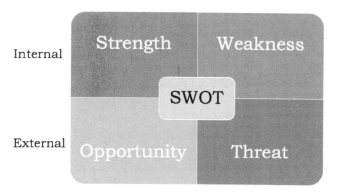

Figure 11.1. SWOT Chart
Source: **Courtesy of Joseph Jones.**

3. *Opportunities*—The potential factors that would allow the organization to improve its situation and relative competitive position among competition and outside pressures.
4. *Threats*—The future external factors that may reduce the organization's relative competitive position due to outside influences within or outside of the organization's span of control (ProvenModels, 2019).

One primary reason that we suggest using a SWOT analysis is its simplicity and potential when done correctly. But SWOT alone is not enough; it must be coupled with processes that break away from traditional or conventional thinking (Brandenburger, 2019).

Another powerful reason to use this tool is that it lends itself to brainstorming, unearthing possibilities, and creatively pursuing untethered ideas, all things that engage teams as they tackle problems of practice and create theories of action to move forward, perfect for uncovering needs when hiring, among other important work. SWOT is a powerful tool, and it doesn't require an MBA to put into practice. It does require focus and specific skill development to do with efficacy.

Focused

The relatively simple SWOT process requires leaders to evaluate their schools in specific contexts. The *Strengths* aspect of the model prompts teams to identify what sets them apart from other institutions, either as a whole or given an adopted practice. In essence, the team works to uncover what makes them superior, such as how well students are learning the curriculum or how strong the relationships are in each classroom. Next, focusing on *Weaknesses* is never easy because so many areas are interconnected and directly related to one another.

Schools should cautiously identify weaknesses to unveil the root cause and not the symptoms. Simply acknowledging weakness does not guarantee success, yet correctly identifying each and knowing all potential weak points puts the team in a better position to plan ahead and make necessary adjustments (Maxwell, 2013). Both the *Strengths* and *Weaknesses* quadrants, once identified, reflect the internal facets of the school, those particulars that are directly within the control of the organization. Great school leaders know the critical importance of having a pulse on their schools and keenly being aware of what is and is not working.

This knowledge provides the insight necessary to successfully navigate change and the school community. The *S* and the *W* keep those critical areas at the forefront of decision-making as information is filtered down into useful and practical next steps toward the desired outcome. In the case of recruitment, an analysis of strengths and weaknesses leads the team toward the right candidates and the best fit for the school. Without this type of analysis, we tend to make uninformed, ill-informative, and subjective decisions.

The *Opportunities* and *Threats* sections of the analysis consider external factors that schools can either use to their benefit or identify as troublesome issues that may adversely impact the school. The objective is to use all of the information collected to strategically move forward. Consider our Pembroke High School fable; the community's economic situation was a "threat" to the school in many ways, which ranged from residents leaving the area to reduced funding. Identifying the threats puts the school in a proactive position to deal with the problems by reaching out to community members, working with legislators, and keeping students at the forefront of policies. This is the meaning of school–community partnerships and bridges relationships for the betterment of students.

Taking this further, as the economic situation steadily improved within the Pembroke community and new businesses emerged, the school recognized the *Opportunities* and embraced STEM as a major initiative that directly impacted recruiting. Within the scope of recruiting, under the umbrella of hiring, SWOT can systematically guide school leaders in their analysis of each candidate to select the best fit in terms of the needs of the school in its current situation. This is often done through well-developed questions and a skillful team of people.

Selection Committee Skill Development

SWOT is a useful, proven analysis tool that is relatively simple to learn. Nonetheless, like all tools, it must be used appropriately among team members in order to be effective. Schools need to understand the intricacies of the tool to be able to employ it as a strategy to determine the best candidate for any given opening on staff. SWOT helps uncover the right fit to complement the makeup of the school.

We've described the power and importance of having skilled hiring selection committees, and these teams can use SWOT as a tool to identify the various skills, traits, and qualities of the person whom they are looking to hire. Being keenly aware of the position that needs to be filled, the roles and responsibilities that the individual will need to possess, and the special attributes that he or she needs to bring will allow the team to hire someone who will add value to the existing team.

Selection committees are often formed based on each person's talents and the role the person plays so that the team is balanced. This is the intersection between intellect and intuition, which is where great results can be found in terms of team dynamics. As Wahl (2013) writes, "Intellect without intuition is a smart person without impact. Intuition without intellect is a spontaneous person without progress" (p. 97). Typically, selection teams comprise individuals within a school who are highly skilled and well respected; most often, these teams also include newer staff members who demonstrate great promise.

The key is to balance the team with expertise as well as raw instinct. But "instinct" is not always as intuitive as we might think. Selection teams must be strengthened in their ability to make appropriate decisions. Because "judgment and learning are calibrated by working alongside a more experienced partner" (Brown, Roediger, & McDaniel, 2014), the balance between experience and impulse must be carefully considered. The key is that both intellect and inclination are necessary. But intellect and instinct are calibrated through skill development, and only experience can guide a selection team through actual selection experiences and professional development to specifically strengthen our ability to interview and discern excellence.

These experiences and professional learning, provided to the selection team, enhance everyone's individual interview skills. This is imperative so that everyone is clear on what distinguishes the best candidate from the rest of the pool. After forming a strong team of experienced leaders and those who show aptitude, the next step is to review all of the important aspects of the interview process, from archetypes to interview questions. The team should be clear on the definition of an "incredible interview experience" and even how prospective candidates should respond to scenarios and prompts.

The team should be guided by a well-developed rubric and a systematic process to glean and evaluate the information that is presented during the layers of the program. To strengthen the interview process, the committee should be consistent and reliable with their evaluation of the responses to each of the candidates. This is achieved through training and maintaining alignment between the interview and the areas identified through the SWOT analysis (see Leadership Team Activity 4).

Too often during interviews, the team is unable to tell the difference between highly talented candidates and everyone else. This is because of ambiguity and a lack of clear strategy for what the team needs and what they should be looking for within the talent pool. The selection committee must be prepared to use interview best practices, some of which we have already described, but also needs to be clear on what they should ideally hear and observe from each question or scenario posed to the candidates throughout the process.

To further develop this skill, teams must have a strong inter-rater reliability, which "essentially refers to the relative consistency of the judgments that are made of the same stimulus by two or more raters" (Lavrakas, 2008). One way to ensure inter-rater reliability is to use SWOT as demonstrated in Leadership Team Activity 4. Developing the team's capacity to conduct quality interviews, grounded in a team of experienced and novice selection committee members, enhances their ability to identify the right candidate for the job.

LEADERSHIP TEAM ACTIVITY 4: SWOT

Schools are the earth's epicenter when it comes to the formation of committees. In education the motto everyone quickly learns is: "When in doubt, form a committee." All joking aside, many of the committees that we form represent the dynamic nature of school, which allows for a deep representation of ideas to flourish. They are designed to solve a myriad of challenges that schools face, from garnering support and resources for student activities to a process for developing a new and responsive master schedule with innovative offerings, including a robust course catalog.

In fact, the willingness of staff to serve on various teams and collaborate with one another is a testament to their dedication in providing the best experiences for students. The power, though, of committee work lies within everyone's ability to work together effectively, which, in turn, taps into the unique perspective of each representative.

> Collaborative decision-making involves bringing together the people who have direct contract or responsibility over the resulting factors of the decision being made and working together toward a common understanding of the next steps in solving a problem or carrying out the initiative. (Jones & Vari, 2019, p. 51)

One such committee that relies on effective collaboration and has evolved from the traditional department chair meeting is the steering committee.

Although throughout this book we refer to developing a strong leadership team, we consider this to be analogous to the proven steering committees that some schools have in place.

This influential committee is most beneficial when comprising individuals who are heavily vested in their own department or group, as well as the overall outcomes that the entire organization is poised to achieve (Harvard Business Essentials, 2004, p. 29). Developed thoughtfully, the adults on the committee should fully represent the diversity of the school, the various departments, student services, and any other related programs that comprise the school as a system.

Steering committees are designed to leverage the unique voice of the individual members through the interspersing of several ideas and thoughts to solve issues, wrestle with dilemmas, and route the school toward successfully meeting its goals. In schools, the principal typically serves as the leader of the committee and provides the structure and support needed for a high-functioning team. The principal position is daunting and riddled with challenges that can derail the best administrator from successfully leading in any number of the capacities in which he or she is charged. The reality of the role requires administrators to rely on a core group of teachers to ensure that the school remains focused on its goals, even when the principal must take his or her eye away from the prize, if even for a glimpse at something that might distract even the strongest leader.

This relationship between the principal as *the leader* and the committee as *the leaders* is grounded in quality communication and forged through transparent, difficult conversations designed to improve the interdependent parts of the school. These leadership teams need to comprise well-informed teacher leaders and other staff who can successfully guide and influence key short- and long-term decisions. "The success of teachers work with students is heavily influenced by the structures of the school and the opportunities available for them and their students . . . the voice of teachers is essential in ensuring these policies and programs are designed in an optimal manner" (Danielson, 2006, pp. 61 and 62). Teacher voice is essential, and great leaders make it their responsibility to not only hear from teachers but also strengthen their voice through skill development exercises.

Successful teams achieve their results through leveraging their strengths and understanding the unique role that each individual plays within the context of coming together for shared decision-making. This is most powerfully done when teams thrive in an environment that is structured to get to the root cause of the issues to unveil key solutions. Using a tool such as the SWOT guides the group around critical topics by providing a formula with sound questioning. Using this tool with the variety of data that schools collect can inform conversations to open participants up to more questions and the need for additional data. Data is never the answer to the problem, but it does provide new questions that get to the underlying problems that we're trying to solve in schools. Some of the most common forms of data are as follows:

Student achievement

- Academic performance: grades
- Academic performance: assessments
- Accountability measures: standardized tests
- Enrichment and elective course: participation

School climate

- Average daily attendance
- Chronic absenteeism
- Discipline infractions
- Extracurricular activity participation

These data can be used to answer some of the questions used within a SWOT analysis to guide conversations and dig deeper into school- and district-based problems. The conversations help to marry the quantitative data with much of the important qualitative or anecdotal data that staff can provide based on their experiences with students. Because there is no more important space than the classroom, hiring and recruiting the right person is paramount to success. When looking at hiring key personnel, the process can be guided by important questions that can govern the discussion within the leadership team.

The information garnered can then be used to set the parameters to guide the selection committee to hire the most suitable and skilled candidate. Consider a high school that has recently had two vacancies within its English department, with one teacher retiring and another who relocated. This situation requires the school to fill two vacancies, but a deeper dive into the open positions says much more about hiring than the need to recruit two English teachers.

Two samples are provided to help start the conversation about how to determine the best person for each of the open jobs. The first is a list where SWOT works with an original question and then a deeper one. The second is a quadrant-based set of questions within each section. Both uncover similar trends, and each has its benefits. Your team's preference matters when using a structure such as this one. In these examples, we would first SWOT the open positions and then SWOT each candidate we interview. You can develop your own protocols, questions, and team activities as you see fit.

- Strengths
  - What strengths should a candidate possess?
    - What skills must a candidate possess to complement the existing ELA team?

- Weaknesses
  - What weaknesses currently exist within the department?
    - Which weaknesses within the department might a candidate help to fulfill?
- Opportunities
  - Who are prospective outside candidates?
    - What do we know about student teachers in the school or district?
- Threats
  - What could prevent us from hiring our best candidate?
    - Which local schools are actively seeking ELA candidates?

Strengths	Weaknesses
• What are the characteristics and attributes that the candidate possesses that can contribute to student success?	• What are some of the academic weaknesses on the current team that could be bridged by this person?
• What qualities does the person have that might contribute to the effectiveness of the team?	• How diverse is the team, and does this person help diversify the group?
• Is the individual committed to improving and growing as a teacher?	• Are there academic needs among the students that need to be addressed that this hire could help?
• Does the individual have leadership experiences?	• Are there other needs in other departments that this person can help fulfill?
Opportunities	**Threats**
• What outside positive influences does this person have that can contribute to our school?	• Why might this person choose not to join our team?
• What opportunities do we have outside of the school team that can help this person grow if he or she joins the team?	• Do we have any specific reservations about this person that might threaten our team's success?
• Where are our candidates coming from that might say something about who we are recruiting in this process?	• Once this person is on the team, what points of vulnerability do we need to know about to support his or her acclimation?
• Who would be the best mentor for this person to be successful if hired?	• Who else will be competing for this particular candidate, and why might the candidate choose a competing school over ours?

Some of the questions within the analysis are direct and can be difficult to answer. However, teams must be willing to not only function cooperatively together with a common purpose but also recognize some of the challenges facing the school and accept them as a reality. Too often we want to ignore even some of the more minor details that can escape us without a finer process. Yet when we combine a strong team, the data we collect, and the power of a strategic tool like SWOT, we position ourselves to be successful (Hansen, 2018). The activity is powerful because not only does it help guide the decision-making regarding recruiting, but it also works to strengthen the team and their skills for collaborating, uncovering issues, asking good questions, and finding solutions. That's what winning teams do that sets them apart from everyone else.

Leadership Team Guiding Questions

1. How well does your leadership team function when identifying, grappling with, and solving issues?
2. How well do we filter our data through a series of questions to identify the root causes?
3. How could you employ SWOT as a tool within various departments and for various topics to adopt a formalized process for strategic decision-making?

Chapter 12

A Recruiting Effort That Stands Out

Vision without action is a daydream. Action without vision is a nightmare.

—Croce (2004, p. 3)

Creating a successful school environment through a winning team requires a continual pursuit for great talent to add to your existing crew while simultaneously developing and growing the people who are already on the team. Education is filled with opportunities to develop a person's capacity and help him or her unveil his or her greatest strengths and unleash his or her truest potential. Effective leaders look for talent around every corner to discover possibilities in every person.

STANDING OUT—WHAT ACTIVE RECRUITING LOOKS LIKE IN ACTION

Allow us to introduce you to Nathalie Princilus. Nathalie is an incredible example of the power of a school system's ability to actively recruit an individual with a particular set of skills needed for the school that found her. Once a school is clear on the ideal candidate, the search process becomes clearer than ever before. Nathalie's story winds us through different schools and different ventures that eventually leads to her current role.

Nathalie's story is a great example of a person who is poised to make a difference and the twists and turns that careers can take for the better but only when schools are actively seeking great candidates for specific needs. Once Nathalie was a part of her current district, her potential was reached because they invested in her, developed her career, and allowed her to impact the system in the unique way that only she could produce. It's stories like this that demonstrate the power in *seeking* talent versus *hoping* for it.

Nathalie Princilus is assistant principal at Delcastle Technical High School and is a great example of an individual who was recognized for her talents, given opportunities to develop her skills, and moved productively through a progressive school system into leadership positions. Nathalie's career track is interesting, diverse, and a perfect model for how great things happen when a school is looking for talent and when an individual situates himself or herself for prospective openings. Nathalie's experience started in New Jersey, and after a few years as an elementary education teacher, she and her family decided to move to Delaware. Being impressed with how Delaware was working with developing statewide programming for students with autism, she knew she would find a home in the state and she soon found herself working within the system. Nathalie's desire to serve students, while keeping an open mind, is what always keeps her available for incredible opportunities when they arise. She is the epitome of the phrase "Luck is when preparation meets opportunity." For Nathalie, an exciting opportunity came by way of a conversation with a friend who indicated that St. Georges Technical High School was actively searching for a dynamic learning support coach (LSC). LSCs were becoming more popular as a result of the district's push to create a fully inclusive environment for its students with special education services. The district's approach to inclusivity in special education service delivery was completely aligned with Nathalie's personal philosophy regarding learning in the classroom.

Nathalie's background is all about possibility and the promise of opportunity. Born in Haiti, she experienced firsthand the sacrifice that her parents made to give her and her siblings a better life. In fact, Nathalie's father and mother came to the United States to work and gain citizenship prior to her arrival. Nathalie learned the payoff of sacrifice from her father; because he was the first to come to the United States to work full-time, while attending Rutgers University to earn his degree, despite already having a BA from a university in Haiti, he demonstrated to her what it means *to give up to go up*. He labored long hours for his family with the prospect of a better life. That sacrifice prevented Nathalie from even meeting her father until she was five years old. From her mother, she learned humility. A humble beginning often earns a fruitful means. Her commitment to family is what drives Nathalie today to help others and to let them know that boundaries can be broken regardless of circumstance. The fuel that drives her and what caused her to be interested in special education is her sister, Loretta. Her younger sister of nine years has a developmental disability, which awoke Nathalie to the needs and supports that families must gain in order to provide the best for their children. Nathalie says that she learned early on something that matters to her more than ever even today: "Don't pity the disability, rather empower the person." This passion was quickly recognized by a school system that was looking for particular strengths in a person to join its already-strong team.

Nathalie's desire to serve students was evident, and a forward-thinking district administrator who was changing practices from the inside out caught notice. Dr. David Jezyk, supervisor of special education, quickly saw Nathalie's unique insight into student needs and her ability to dissect psychology reports and actualize the information so that students were best served in the classroom and beyond. Working closely with Nathalie, and revealing the vision of the special education department, Jezyk and his team promoted Nathalie to oversee the Life Skills Program at a sister school, which serves students who are on course to receive an alternative diploma. Nathalie's belief in expressing her values and what is right for students connected perfectly with what Dr. Jezyk and the Delcastle team were looking for in a person to lead a growing department. It's an example of how great systems match their needs to the individual talents of each person on the team so that team members are motivated to be their best self and do their best work.

Nathalie quickly worked with the team to align the curriculum, to guarantee the necessary resources, and to make sure that there was an overall coherence within the program. After three years in the position, Nathalie was moved into a district-level transition specialist role, which oversaw postsecondary transition for all students who qualify for special education services in all four schools within the district. After one short year, an assistant principal position opened at Delcastle, and Nathalie was easily the best fit for the role. Currently, she serves in that capacity, and her background, passion for students, and desire to meet the needs of all learners are evident in her work on a daily basis.

Nathalie's progression is a wonderful example of the cross section between a school's desire to build a winning team and an individual's pursuit of his or her passion. Nathalie's goal to develop her own leadership skills and uncover important possibilities to providing every student with a world-class education was capitalized on by several key leaders who recognized her unique ability to serve students and the greater community. With an aligned vision for services that Nathalie clearly knew how to provide, the match was made in every position that came her way. The District's ability to recognize and grow its leaders is precisely the formula that's leading to the motivation and retention of its top talent, people like Nathalie who we need on the team.

Each school has the opportunity to find an incredible person every time it seeks to fill a vacancy. These critical decisions require schools and districts to position themselves in a way whereby great candidates are attracted to their system because of opportunities and fit. This frame of mind, which we are always searching for great candidates, reinforces our need to constantly promote our brand, reinforce the great work being done, and actively find superstars. Once our superstars are on board, it's our fundamental responsibility to invest in them, uncover their unique talents, and capitalize on their energy and effort.

THE OTHER SIDE OF THE COIN

As schools and districts improve their recruiting efforts and employ innovative incentive practices, it's critical to remember that a meaningful culture and positive working environment are the keys to retaining talent. Great hiring methods are only a third of the talent equation. You need the reputation, you need the lure, and you also need a strategic plan for motivating and inspiring your people to achieve greatness, which we detail in *Retention for a Change*. A powerful example of this is in the use of money, specifically signing bonuses.

Money works well for recruiting teachers, but it's not a great tool for retaining them. "The fact is that money is not as powerful a reward as many people think" (Gostick & Elton, 2007, p. 9). We must find new ways to use money as a recruiting strategy, but we must also recognize that retention is far more than an incentives game. Schools need to be places of inspiration and energy, and it's our daily interactions that lead to retention, not the paycheck.

The impactful incentives that we are advocating focus on recruitment and not performance. We know that teacher shortages are real, and many schools struggle to attract talent even when they're in good supply. That's why the hiring process needs to ramp up with glamor and glory. And once your team is assembled, you have to move into a different gear as a leader, employing the strategies that make our work purposeful, meaningful, and fun. We don't need pay and incentives for performance; we need passionate and invigorating environments. Motivation and retention are different from your recruitment tactics.

We've long known that improved salaries for teachers is a needed strategy to recruiting, but using money for productivity and recognition doesn't work. "Tell people that their income will depend on their productivity or performance rating, and they will focus on the numbers" (Kohn, 1993). This outcome-driven target for teachers is shortsighted, a desperate attempt among educators to improve student achievement reports. The innovation using dollars and cents that we're calling for in education requires more "sense" than dollars.

Let's create environments that entice and attract candidates, and let's be intentional with the open positions and gaps that we can strategically fill by being laser focused. This must be the basis for recruiting and hiring because teachers don't generally go into education for pay. Much of what gets cited as the reasons that teachers leave the profession are not about money but rather the working conditions within our schools. "Things like pay and signing bonuses can entice teachers to particular districts, but support and leadership are what keep them from moving on" (Honaker, 2018).

This is why we advocate for a unique structure in the creation of your team within a *before*, *during*, and *after* model. It's the *after* that keeps them from leaving your school or the profession altogether. To support our teachers, we leverage three influential drivers: motivation, inspiration, and energy at work. In a time when "79 percent of employees who quit their jobs cite a lack of appreciation as a key reason for leaving," we have a great deal of work to do (Gostick & Elton, 2007, p. 8). It's the reason why we wrote *Retention for a Change* as a sequel to *Building a Winning Team*, and as we conclude, you'll see why taking action is the only next step.

Chapter Focus Questions

1. How well do you develop and grow talent within your organization?
2. What practices are in place to help teachers feel a deep connection with the school?
3. Is innovation the norm or the exception?

Chapter 13

Conclusion

Taking Action

You must strive for deep understanding first, ideas second.

—Maddock (2019, p. 105)

Our goal with this work was twofold:

1. We wanted to uncover and reveal the current conditions and issues regarding the reputation that our schools need and the recruitment process that must get ramped up. Our goal was to dig deep into the issues so that you understand the core of the problem so that we create insight before action (Maddock, 2019).
2. We wanted to provide you with specific ideas and action steps that work. Our goal is for you to use the ideas in the book with your leadership teams and adapt them to suit your needs rather than adopting them to fill a void. Although many of the technical tips and leadership team activities can be replicated with little deviation from our recipe, we still encourage you to think hard about your specific problems of practice that you're trying to solve before putting any of them into place.

Fullan's (2019) *Nuance* calls for a new age of leadership with "leaders who see below the surface, grasp hidden patterns, find new pathways to alter and shape better outcomes, and have a burning desire to make things better for the vast majority of people" (p. 11). We agree. Too many of our concerns with the future of education, including teacher shortage, are complex in nature and scope. To solve these issues, we need to go well beyond the surface. Much of what we have outlined in this book may be seen as radical—school branding efforts, culture assessments, housing agreements, teacher bonuses, and more—but the same leadership efforts that got us to this point aren't going to be the ones that change the future (Goldsmith & Reiter, 2007). We have to overcome the status quo and pave the way forward with critical thinking and massive action.

This book is a call to action. We include specifics in the deeper dives, technical tips, and leadership team activities, but change requires action. Our greatest desire is that this book fuels necessary change that equips you to build your winning team. The work doesn't move forward because we've identified a need, pointed to a problem, or admired an issue. It requires a lot of thought and serious planning, but great things are ahead for those who choose to think outside of the box to create an incredible school.

Much of the research that we conducted for this book comes from the business world, organizational leadership, and the worlds of psychology and systems theory. We hope to have organized it into usable parts with ideas that somewhat deviate from educational literature so that the strategies and techniques introduced herein might connect with you in a different and meaningful way. After all, our goal is to challenge the system with a new approach and newly found vigor for building a winning team.

Finally, we love the teaching profession and what education represents for children. Knowing that fewer people are choosing to become teachers is devastating and requires a call to action for everyone in our profession. We leave you with the story of Courtney Wynn, which demonstrates the power of our *BDA R3 Model*—reputation, recruitment, retention—as it comes together perfectly for Principal EL's school in Wilmington. With the right reputation, great recruiting practices, and a motivational environment, Courtney joined the team at Thomas Edison because all three aspects of the model came together perfectly. As you read the story, we hope that it inspires you to do more to build your winning team, and we hope that it piques your interest into our third R of the *BDA R3 Model*—retention, which we address in complete detail within the pages of our forthcoming *Retention for a Change*.

Courtney Wynn was a freshman at Endicott College in Beverly, Massachusetts, when she first heard Principal EL speak. It was her freshman invocation, and EL "did some rapping and other fun stuff to kick us off," she said. At the time, she thought nothing of it. Interestingly, that's not where her journey begins as an education major or an enthused teacher candidate.

Fast forward, only one year later, Courtney saw Principal EL on stage for the second time. She transferred into the education department after deciding to become a teacher during her sophomore year.

Endicott requires education majors to engage in various schools each semester, and Courtney visited a number of schools as a result of her studies. As she listened to Principal EL this time around, she heard his message differently. He told the story about his school, and she imagined a place that was unlike anything she had experienced so far. And unlike her own personal school experience, EL talked about the power of relationships and referred to the school environment as a family. He said that the kids needed him and that he needed them too. He told stories about chess clubs and after-school activities that kept students from a life of crime.

EL described teachers as difference-makers and that a major responsibility of administrators is to give them what they need, "Support your teachers so that they can support the students." Courtney was drawn to EL's message and was deeply impacted by what she heard. She was inspired, and the idea of teaching meant something even greater. She remembered one of his lines that she repeated several times when we interviewed her: "Every child needs someone to be crazy about them." The story was so compelling that she wanted to join Thomas Edison's team no matter what it would take.

After the speech, as 40–50 education majors exited the hall, Courtney approached Principal EL and asked for his business card. She told him that she wanted to student teach at his school, an interesting proposition for a sophomore education major in Massachusetts to student teach in Wilmington, Delaware. Nonetheless, she was bold enough to ask and relentless enough to pursue it. Courtney told us that EL's vision for inner-city schools and the description of the impact one could make were something that she knew she wouldn't get from her traditional placement by the small college in Beverly.

Courtney said that most of the schools she visited were filled with students who were ready for school, were positioned to learn, and certainly didn't need programs to keep them engaged rather than fall prey to the dangers of their own neighborhoods. She called it "selfish," but she wanted to be needed by the school community, to make a lasting impact on students through teaching and guidance. We don't consider this selfish at all; we consider it a calling, a desire so deep, fueled by passion and purpose, to change a child's life forever. That's the power of a teacher.

As some time passed, Courtney e-mailed Principal EL to inquire about a student teaching placement for her senior year. She wanted to be proactive, knowing this was an unusual request. She told us that she wanted to connect with teaching the way that EL had described in his story, on a deep level, through "love and safety," inside the school walls but also beyond the school day and into the community. But Principal EL didn't respond to her e-mail. She guessed he wasn't sure about the logistics or maybe he thought she was crazy. But she didn't stop there. She went to the president of Endicott College to endorse her student teaching placement in Wilmington, and they e-mailed Principal EL together. That's what sealed the deal.

Courtney was required by the college to complete a semester-long student teaching during her senior year. She was able to set it up so that the college was connected with Thomas Edison, and she was granted permission to teach in a first-grade classroom. But she had other logistical challenges to overcome. She needed a place to live, she needed transportation, and she told us that she was a bit scared. She asked her sister, Kaylie Wynn, to join her on the journey in Delaware. Through fate, good luck, and definitely a token of goodwill, Kaylie's boss granted her leave with a job when she returned. Courtney used her college room and board money toward an apartment in Newark, a college town adjacent to Wilmington. She, her sister, and their two dogs, Tucker and Mason, made the trek south, found an apartment, a couple of part-time jobs, and the rest is history. Courtney completed a semester of student teaching at Thomas Edison and returned to Endicott to finish her senior year.

Later that year, Principal EL was at the college again to speak to another group of students, and he asked Courtney to join him to tell her story about her experiences at his school. That night, EL and the education department went to dinner, and Courtney was invited to join them. EL and Courtney talked about where she wanted to teach. She was contemplating Teach for America, seeing that as a vehicle to join a high-needs school. EL told her about an opening he had due to a maternity leave situation where the teacher wasn't going to return. It was a first-grade teaching position, similar to her student teaching role. Soon thereafter, Courtney went to Wilmington on her spring break to sign the paperwork.

Courtney Wynn still teaches at Thomas Edison Charter School in Wilmington. She's in her fifth year as we write the final pages of this book in 2019. Courtney remains inspired to stay in the city school because of the connections that the school makes with students and the connections she has with the staff. She told us that it truly is a family environment where everyone truly is "crazy" about kids. She's involved in tutoring and other aspects of the job that allow her to make a little extra money by being involved with students beyond the school day. She calls Principal EL her "Delaware dad" and says that he lives what he preaches. The students call Courtney their "school mom."

Courtney's story reveals that there are incredible people out there who want to make a difference in students' lives in a big way. She told us a story about an aggressive student whom she supported with a simple piece of paper. She told him to trace an infinite symbol whenever he got upset. She said, "Forever and always—I believe in you that much—infinite." It calmed the student and allowed him to access school in a successful way. Wynn said it was "unreal." She said that if she could "impact just one student in a positive way each year, it was enough to continue to stay at the school."

The truth is that Thomas Edison embodies many of the key ideas featured throughout this book. As practitioners, we see potential in every hire we bring on board to make a lasting impact on the students we teach. Courtney feels that the school invests in her with professional development and career opportunities that develop the whole teacher, equipping her to truly influence her students. The school treats teachers as experts and challenges them to put precision into practice. The depth of Courtney Wynn's story demonstrates clearly that our reputation is what matters when we want to attract the most passionate people; our efforts to recruit in new ways at dinners and during spring breaks are the difference-makers; and our school culture regarding motivation, inspiration, and energy retains the best people on our winning teams.

References

Ahn, T., & Vigdor, J. (2011). *Making teacher incentives work: Lessons from North Carolina's teacher bonus program.*

Altman, J. (2017). Don't be surprised when your employees quit. *Forbes.* Retrieved from https://www.forbes.com/sites/valleyvoices/2017/02/22/dont-be-surprised-when-your-employees-quit/#575dcb06325e.

Anderson, M. (2016). *Learning to choose, choosing to learn: The key to student motivation and achievement.* Alexandria, VA: ASCD.

Baggarly, A. (2011). *A band of misfits: Tales of the 2010 San Francisco Giants.* Chicago: Triumph Books.

Bandura, A. (1995). *Self-efficacy in changing societies.* New York, NY: Cambridge University Press.

Bergman, J. L., & Schuler, T. (1992, December). Teaching at-risk students to read strategically. Retrieved from http://www.ascd.org/publications/educational_leadership/dec92/vol50/num04/Teaching_At-Risk_Students_To_Read_Strategically.aspx.

Bernhardt, V. (1999). *The school portfolio: A comprehensive framework for school improvement.* New York, NY: Taylor & Francis.

Blair, J. (2000, August 2). Districts wooing teachers with bonuses, incentives. Retrieved from https://www.edweek.org/ew/articles/2000/08/02/43raid.h19.html.

Blanchard, K., & Muchnick, M. (2003). *The leadership pill: The missing ingredient in motivating people today.* New York, NY: Free Press.

Blase, J., & Blase, J. (2004). *Handbook of instructional leadership: How successful principals promote teaching and learning.* Thousand Oaks, CA: Corwin Press.

Bock, L. (2015). *Work rules: Insights from inside Google that will transform how you live and lead.* New York, NY: Twelve Hachette Book Group.

Brabant, T. (2010, October). The simple genius of checklists. Retrieved from https://www.boeing.com/news/frontiers/archive/2010/october/i_bca05.pdf.

Brandenburger, A. (2019). Are your company's strengths really weaknesses? *Harvard Business Review.* https://hbr.org/2019/08/are-your-companys-strengths-really-weaknesses.

Brown, P. C., Roediger, H. L., & McDaniel, M. A. (2014). *Make it stick: The science of successful learning.* Cambridge, MA: Belknap Press.

Browne, S. (2017). *HR on purpose: Developing deliberate people passion.* Danvers, MA: Society for Human Resource Management.

Bryant, A. (2018). How to hire the right person. *The New York Times.* Retrieved from https://www.nytimes.com/guides/business/how-to-hire-the-right-person.

Buckingham, M., & Coffman, C. (1999). *First break all the rules: What the world's greatest managers do differently.* New York, NY: Simon & Schuster.

Carroll T. G., Fulton, K., Abercrombie, K., & Yoon, I. (2004). *Fifty years after Brown v. Board of Education: A two-tiered education system.* Washington, DC: National Commission on Teaching and America's Future.

Carroll, K. (2004). *The rules of the red rubber ball.* New York, NY: Hyperion.

Carver-Thomas, D., & Darling-Hammond, L. (2017). *Teacher turnover: Why it matters and what we can do about it.* Palo Alto, CA: Learning Policy Institute.

Casas, J. (2017). Culturize. San Diego: Dave Burgess Consulting, Inc.

Coleman, J., & Whitehurst, J. (2014). 3 priorities for leaders who want to go beyond command-and-control. *Harvard Business Review.* https://hbr.org/2014/05/3-priorities-for-leaders-who-want-to-go-beyond-command-and-control.

Collins, J. (2001). *Good to great: Why some companies make the leap . . . and others don't.* New York, NY: Harper Business.

Collins, J. C., & Porras, J. I. (1994). *Built to last: Successful habits of visionary companies.* New York, NY: HarperCollins.

Colón, L. (2017). Your guide to running a school like Disney. EdSurge. Retrieved from https://www.edsurge.com/news/2017-04-26-your-guide-to-running-a-school-like-disney-world.

Commission on Public Schools. (2016). Guide to developing core values, beliefs, and learning expectations. Retrieved from https://cpss.neasc.org/sites/cpss.neasc.org/files/Downloads_pdf/Guide%20to%20Developing%20Core%20Values.pdf.

Coyle, D. (2012). *The little book of talent.* New York, NY: Random House.

Coyle, D. (2018). *The culture code: The secrets to highly successful groups.* New York, NY: Random House.

Croce, P. (2004). *Lead or get off the pot! The seven secrets of a self-made leader.* New York, NY: Fireside.

Dagdeviren, O. (2015). *Creative hiring: The pinnacle model for spontaneous, imaginative, collaborative interviews.* London: Ozan Dagdeviren.

Danielson, C. (2006). *Teacher leadership that strengthens professional practice.* Alexandria, VA: ASCD.

Darling-Hammond, L. (2013). *Getting teacher evaluation right: What really matters for effectiveness and improvement.* New York, NY: Teachers College Press.

Darling-Hammond, L., Hyler, M. E., & Gardner, M. (2017). Effective teacher professional development. Retrieved from https://learningpolicyinstitute.org/product/effective-teacher-professional-development-brief.

Daskal, L. (2017). *The leadership gap: What gets between you and your greatness.* New York, NY: Penguin.

Davis, S. (2018). *Getting to us: How great coaches make great teams.* New York, NY: Penguin.

Dilan, E. (2018, April 12). Organizational values: The most underutilized corporate asset. Retrieved from https://www.forbes.com/sites/forbescoachescouncil/2018/04/12/organizational-values-the-most-underutilized-corporate-asset/#33b7325d52a3.

Di Stefano, G., Gino, F., Pisano, G. P., & Staats, B. R. (2014). Making experience count: The role of reflection in individual learning. Retrieved from https://papers.ssrn.com/sol3/papers.cfm?abstract_id=2414478##.

Downey, C. J., Steffy, B. E., English, F. W., Frase, L. W., & Poston, W. K. (2004). *The three-minute classroom walk-through: Changing school supervisory practice one teacher at a time*. Thousand Oaks, CA: Corwin Press.

Duckworth, A. (2016). *Grit: The power of passion and perseverance*. New York, NY: Scribner.

DuFour, R. (2004). *Whatever it takes: How professional learning communities respond when kids don't learn*. Bloomington, IN: Solution Tree. United States: National Educational Service.

DuFour, R., & Marzano, R. (2011). *Leaders of learning: How districts, schools, and classroom leaders improve student achievement*. Bloomington, IN: Solution Tree.

Dweck, C. (2008). *Mindset: The new psychology of success*. New York, NY: Ballantine Books.

Earley, P. C., & Mosakowski, E. (2004). Cultural intelligence. *Harvard Business Review*. https://hbr.org/2004/10/cultural-intelligence.

Education Next. (2018, June 13). EdStat: $18 billion a year is spent on professional development for U.S. teachers. Retrieved from https://www.educationnext.org/edstat-18-billion-year-spent-professional-development-u-s-teachers/.

Elmore, R. F., & City, E. (2007, May/June). The road to school improvement. Retrieved from http://hepg.org/hel-home/issues/23_3/helarticle/the-road-to-school-improvement_229.

Espinoza, D., Saunders, R., Kini, T., & Darling-Hammond, L. (2018). *Taking the long view: State efforts to solve teacher shortages by strengthening the profession*. Palo Alto, CA: Learning Policy Institute.

Francais, (2014). Forty Years Later: The Extraordinary River Blindness Partnership Sets Its Sights on New Goals. (2014, July/August). Retrieved from http://www.worldbank.org/en/news/feature/2014/07/03/forty-years-later-the-extraordinary-river-blindness-partnership-sets-its-sights-on-new-goals.

Fullan, M. (2014). *The principal: Three keys to maximizing impact*. San Francisco, CA: Jossey-Bass.

Fullan, M. (2019). *Nuance: Why some leaders succeed and others fail*. Thousand Oaks, CA: Corwin Press.

Gassam, J. (2018). The best places to work for 2019. Forbes.com. Retrieved from https://www.forbes.com/sites/janicegassam/2018/12/07/the-best-places-to-work-for-2019/#3aa1686f528f.

Godin, S. (2018). *This is marketing: You can't be seen until you learn to see*. New York, NY: Penguin.

Goldsmith, M., & Reiter, M. (2007). *What got you here won't get you there: How successful people become even more successful*. New York, NY: Hyperion.

Goldstein, D. (2019, January 4). The fight to keep teachers in tech hubs from being priced out. Retrieved from https://www.nytimes.com/2019/01/04/us/teachers-priced-out-tech-hubs.html.

Goleman, D., Boyatzis, R. E., & McKee, A. (2002). *Primal leadership: Realizing the power of emotional intelligence*. Boston: Harvard Business School Press.

Gordon, J. (2009). *Training camp: A fable about excellence*. Hoboken, NJ: John Wiley & Sons, Inc.

Gordon, J. (2018). *The power of a positive team: Proven principles and practices that make great teams great*. Hoboken, NJ: John Wiley & Sons, Inc.

Gostick, A., & Elton, C. (2007). *The carrot principle: How the best managers use recognition to engage their people, retain talent, and accelerate performance*. New York, NY: Simon & Schuster.

Graber, S. (2015). 9 employee engagement archetypes. *Harvard Business Review*. Retrieved from https://hbr.org/visual-library/2015/12/9-employee-engagement-archetypes.

Gwande, A. (2009). *The checklist manifesto*. New York, NY: Henry Holt and Company.

Hansen, M. (2018). *Great at work: How top performers do less, work better, and achieve more*. New York, NY: Simon & Schuster.

Harnish, V. (2014). *Scaling up: Mastering the Rockefeller habits 2.0. How a few companies make it . . . and why the rest don't*. Chicago: Gazelles, Inc.

Harvard Business Essentials. (2004). *Managing projects large and small: The fundamental skills for delivering on budget and on time*. Boston, MA: Harvard Business School Publishing.

Hattie, J. (2009). *Visible learning: A synthesis of over 800 meta-analyses relating to achievement*. London: Routledge.

Haun, L. (2013, January 14). Don't hire the perfect candidate. Retrieved from https://hbr.org/2013/01/dont-hire-the-perfect-candidat.

Hernandez, N. (2018, November 5). Michigan teachers cash in on housing incentives. Retrieved from https://www.apnews.com/2d13d396b75543f18ab0670d390af349.

Hewlett, S. A., Marshall, M., & Sherbin, L. (2013). How diversity can drive innovation. Retrieved from https://hbr.org/2013/12/how-diversity-can-drive-innovation.

Hirsch, J. (2018). This 1 interview test reveals a candidate's true character and it only takes seconds: The "wrapper test" reveals a lot about job candidates—without them even saying a word. Retrieved from https://www.inc.com/joe-hirsch/how-to-tell-if-your-next-hire-has-character-even-before-interview-begins.html.

Honaker, A. (2018, April 30). Bonuses might get teachers to a district, but what makes them want to stay? Retrieved from https://www.macon.com/news/local/education/article209781254.html.

Huang, G. (2018, March 22). *5 Reasons you should attend a virtual career fair*. Retrieved from https://www.forbes.com/sites/georgenehuang/2018/03/22/5-reasons-you-should-attend-a-virtual-career-fair/#2b3ec2f59d3e.

Huffington, A. (2014). *Thrive: The third metric to redefining success and creating a life of well-being, wisdom, and wonder*. New York, NY: Crown.

Human Resource Executive. (2018, July/August). Creating a culture of "engagement every day" at a major North American retailer. http://www.humanresourceexecutive-digital.com/humanresourceexecutive/june_2018?pg=27#pg27.

Ingersoll, R., & May, H. (2016). Minority teacher recruitment, employment, and retention: 1987 to 2013. Learning Policy Institute, September 15, 2016. Retrieved from https://learningpolicyinstitute.org/product/minority-teacher-recruitment-brief.

Johnson, S. M., Berg, J. H., & Donaldson, M. L. (2005). *Who stays in teaching and why? A review of the literature on teacher retention.* Washington, DC: National Retired Teachers Association.

Jones, J., & Vari, T. (2019). *Candid and compassionate feedback: Transforming everyday practice in schools.* New York, NY: Routledge.

Knowledge@Wharton. (2018, October 22). *The student debt crisis: Could it slow the U.S. economy?* Retrieved from http://knowledge.wharton.upenn.edu/article/student-loan-debt-crisis/.

Kohn, A. (1993). Why incentive plans cannot work. *Harvard Business Review.* https://hbr.org/1993/09/why-incentive-plans-cannot-work.

Kotter, J. P. (2012). *Leading change.* Boston, MA: Harvard Business Review Press.

Kotter, J. P. (2014). *Accelerate: Building strategic agility for a faster-moving world.* Boston, MA: Harvard Business School Publishing.

Lavrakas, P. (2008). Encyclopedia of survey research methods. Retrieved from http://methods.sagepub.com/reference/encyclopedia-of-survey-research-methods/n236.xml.

Learning Forward. (n.d.). Redesign PD community cycle of inquiry. Retrieved from https://learningforward.org/learning-opportunities/redesign-pd-community-of-practice/cycle-of-inquiry.

LeeYohn, D. (2018). *Fusion: How integrating brand and culture powers the world's greatest companies.* London: Hachette.

Lemov, D. (2015). *Teach like a champion 2.0: 62 techniques that put students on the path to college.* San Francisco, CA: Jossey-Bass.

Lencioni, P. (2016). *The ideal team player: How to recognize and cultivate the three essential virtues.* Hoboken, NJ: John Wiley & Sons, Inc.

Loewus, L. (2018, January 23). Does it make sense to offer housing perks for teachers? Some question whether providing housing for teachers is sound public policy. Retrieved from https://www.edweek.org/ew/articles/2018/01/24/does-it-make-sense-to-offer-housing.html.

Long, M. (2018, February 28). 5 ways to reach educators on social media. Retrieved from https://www.adweek.com/digital/5-ways-to-reach-educators-on-social-media/.

Maddock, M. (2019). *Plan D: How to dream, drive and deliver.* Charleston, SC: Advantage Media Group.

Marzano, R. J., Pickering, D. J., & Pollock, J. E. (2001). *Classroom instruction that works: Research-based strategies for increasing student achievement.* Alexandria, VA: ASCD.

Marzano, R. J., & Waters, T. (2009). *District leadership that works: Striking the right balance.* Bloomington, IN: Solution Tree Press.

Marzano, R. J., Waters, T., & McNulty B. A. (2005). *School leadership that works: From research to results.* Aurora, CO: Mid-continent Research for Education and Learning.

Mauboussin, M.J. (2012). The true measures of success. *Harvard Business Review.* https://hbr.org/2012/10/the-true-measures-of-success.

Maxwell, J. (1998). *The 21 irrefutable laws of leadership: Follow them and people will follow you.* Nashville, TN: Thomas Nelson.

Maxwell, J. (2013). *Sometimes you win sometimes you learn: Life's greatest lessons are gained from our losses.* New York, NY: Hachette Book Group.

McCord, P. (2018, January–February). How to hire. Retrieved from https://hbr.org/2018/01/how-to-hire.

McKeown, G. (2014, March 3). Hire slow, fire fast. Retrieved from https://hbr.org/2014/03/hire-slow-fire-fast.

Merck Offers Free Distribution of New River Blindness Drug. (1987, October 22). Retrieved from https://www.nytimes.com/1987/10/22/world/merck-offers-free-distribution-of-new-river-blindness-drug.html.

Miller, D. (2017). *Building a story brand: Clarify your message so customers will listen.* Nashville, TN: HarperCollins.

Miller, M. (2018). *Talent magnet: How to attract and keep the best people.* Oakland, CA: Berrett-Koehler Publishers, Inc.

Murphy, M. (2012). *Hiring for attitude: A revolutionary approach to recruiting star performers with both tremendous skills and superb attitude.* New York, NY: McGraw-Hill.

National Association of Secondary School Principals. (2011). *National Association of Secondary School Principals Breaking Ranks: The Comprehensive Framework for School Improvement.* Reston, VA: NASSP. https://www.principalsmonth.org/igx_temp/nassp_leading_success/Mod_1_Act_1_Reading_BRFramework ExecSummary.pdf.

NFL. (2019). The rules of the draft. Retrieved from https://operations.nfl.com/the-players/the-nfl-draft/the-rules-of-the-draft/.

Ogilvy, D. (1983). Ogilvy on advertising. Retrieved from https://www.academia.edu/34876497/Ogilvy_on_Advertising.

Page, B. (2014). 5 reasons to hire slow and 5 reasons to fire fast. Retrieved from https://www.inc.com/bubba-page/5-reasons-to-hire-slow-and-5-reasons-to-fire-fast.html.

Passy, J. (2018, February 14). Fewer Americans are majoring in education, but will students pay the price? Retrieved from https://www.marketwatch.com/story/fewer-americans-are-majoring-in-education-but-will-students-pay-the-price-2018-02-14.

Paterson, J. (2018). Closing the diversity gap: New research sheds light on how to inspire, recruit and retain teachers of color. *Teaching Tolerance* (60), Fall. https://www.tolerance.org/magazine/fall-2018/closing-the-diversity-gap.

Perry, D. E., & Haluska, M. J. (2016). *Hiring greatness: How to recruit your dream team and crush the competition.* Hoboken, NJ: John Wiley & Sons, Inc.

Peterson-DeLuca, A. (2016). Top five qualities of effective teachers, according to students. Pearson. Retrieved from https://www.pearsoned.com/top-five-qualities-effective-teachers/.

Peyre, S. E. (2014). CRICO operating room team training collaborative: Closed loop communication. Retrieved from https://www.rmf.harvard.edu/Clinician-Resources/Article/2014/CRICO-Operating-Room-Team-Training-Collaborative-Closed-Loop-Communication.

ProvenModels. (2019). Retrieved from https://www.provenmodels.com/37/swot-analysis/c.-roland-christensen--edmund-p.-learned--kenneth-r.-andrews--william-d.-guth.

Rabe, C. B. (2006). *The innovation killer: How what we know limits what we can imagine—and what smart companies are doing about it.* New York, NY: American Management Association.

Ravitch, D. (2010). *The death and life of the great American school system: How testing and choice are undermining education.* New York, NY: Basic Books.

Reeves, D. (2009). *Leading change in your school: How to conquer myths, build commitment, and get results.* Alexandria, VA: ASCD.

Reynolds, A., & Lewis, D. (2017, March 30). Teams solve problems faster when they're more cognitively diverse. Retrieved from https://hbr.org/2017/03/teams-solve-problems-faster-when-theyre-more-cognitively-diverse.

Robinson, A. (2017). *The best team wins: Build your business through predictive hiring.* Austin, TX: Greanleaf Book Group Press.

Rodriguez, D. (2017). Why the right candidate isn't responding to your job ad. Retrieved from https://www.forbes.com/sites/forbeshumanresourcescouncil/2017/12/28/why-the-right-candidate-isnt-responding-to-your-job-ad/#38a10bc86f8e.

Sackett, T. (2018). *The talent fix: A leader's guide to recruiting great talent.* Alexandria, VA: Society of Human Resources.

Sanders, W., & Rivers, J. (1996, November). Cumulative and residual effects of teachers on future student academic achievement. *Sociology of Education, 70,* 256–284.

Scheerens, J., & Bosker, R. (1997). *The foundations of educational effectiveness.* New York, NY: Pergamon.

Scheiber, N., & Wingfield, N. (2017, August 2). Amazon's job fair sends clear message: Now hiring thousands. Retrieved from https://www.nytimes.com/2017/08/02/technology/amazons-jobs-fair-sends-clear-message-now-hiring-thousands.html.

Schmoker, M. (2006). *Results now: How we can achieve unprecedented improvements in teaching and learning.* Alexandria, VA: ASCD.

Schoemaker, P. (2015, January 28). The right way to do a SWOT analysis. Retrieved from https://www.inc.com/paul-schoemaker/12-tips-swot-analysis.html.

Schrage, M., & Kiron, D. (2018, June 26). Leading with next-generation key performance indicators. Retrieved from https://sloanreview.mit.edu/projects/leading-with-next-generation-key-performance-indicators/.

Self, J. (2019, January 17). This SC school district has a plan to keep teachers around—a $5,000 annual bonus. https://www.thestate.com/news/local/education/article224673070.html.

Shapiro, E. (2018, October 11). Bonuses of up to $8,000 to teach in struggling New York schools. Retrieved from https://www.nytimes.com/2018/10/11/nyregion/nyc-teachers-union-contract.html.

Sinanis, T., & Sanfelippo, J. (2015). *The power of branding your school: Telling your school's story.* Thousand Oaks, CA: Corwin Press.

Sinek, S. (2009). *Start with why: How great leaders inspire everyone to take action.* New York, NY: Penguin.

Smart, G., & Street, R. (2008). *Who.* New York, NY: Random House.

Smith, S., Chavez, A., & Seaman, G. (2017). *Cognitive growth targets questioning flipbook*. Modern Teacher.

Society for Human Resources Management. (2016). The new talent landscape: Recruiting difficulty and skills shortages. Retrieved from https://www.shrm .org/hr-today/trends-and-forecasting/research-and-surveys/Documents/SHRM%20 New%20Talent%20Landscape%20Recruiting%20Difficulty%20Skills.pdf.

Strong, J. H. (2018). *Qualities of effective teachers* (3rd ed.). Alexandria, VA: ASCD.

Strong, J. H., Ward, T. J., & Grant, L. W. (2011). What makes good teachers good? A cross-case analysis of the connection between teacher effectiveness and student achievement. *Journal of Teacher Education, 62*(4), 339–355. doi:10.1177/0022487111404241.

Sutcher, L., Darling-Hammond, L., & Carver-Thomas, D. (2016). *A coming crisis in teaching? Teacher supply, demand, and shortages in the U.S.* Palo Alto, CA: Learning Policy Institute.

Tarpey, M. (2018, July 25). How to write better job descriptions. Retrieved from https://resources.careerbuilder.com/recruiting/solutions/writing-job-advertisements.

Taylor, B. (2011). Don't let what you know limit what you imagine. *Harvard Business Review*. https://hbr.org/2011/11/dont-let-what-you-know-limit-w.

Thaler, L. K., & Koval, R. (2009). *The power of small: Why little things make all the difference*. New York, NY: Random House.

Thomas-EL, S., Jones, J., & Vari, T. (2020). *Passionate leadership: Creating a culture of success in every school*. Thousand Oaks, CA: Corwin Press.

Trimarco, G. (2017). Overcoming the "hire a warm body" mentality. Retrieved from https://www.forbes.com/sites/forbescoachescouncil/2017/06/13/overcoming-the-hire-a-warm-body-mentality/#2410d7e490c9.

Wahl, E. (2013). *Unthink: Rediscover your creative genius*. Danvers, MA, United States: Crown Publishing Group.

Waitzkin, J. (2007). *An inner journey to optimal performance: The art of learning*. New York, NY: Free Press.

Walsh, K., Putnam, H., & Lewis, A. (2015, May). *Attract the best teachers to schools that need them most*. Retrieved from https://www.nctq.org/dmsView/NCTQ_-_Standard_13_Fine_Points_-_Attracting_Best_Teachers_to_Schools_That_Need_Them.

Whitaker, T., Whitaker, B., & Lumpa, D. (2009). *Motivating and inspiring teachers: The educational leader's guide for building staff morale*. New York, NY: Routledge.

Whitaker, T., Zoul, J., & Casas J. (2017). *Start. Right. Now.: Teach and lead for excellence*. San Diego, CA: Dave Burgess Consulting, Inc.

Whitehurst, G. J. (2002, March). Scientifically based research on teacher quality: Research on teacher preparation and professional development. White House Conference on Preparing Tomorrow's Teachers. Retrieved from http://citeseerx.ist.psu .edu/viewdoc/download?doi=10.1.1.468.8079&rep=rep1&type=pdf.

Wilson, D., & Conyers, M. (2016). *Teaching students to drive their brains: Metacognitive strategies, activities, and lesson ideas*. Alexandria, VA: ASCD.

Wintrip, S. (2017). *High velocity highering: How to hire top talent in an instant*. Columbus, OH: McGraw-Hill Education.

Index